—BUCHAN—
Land of Plenty

Sc (1xr2)

For Rachel, Daniel, Hannah,
Katy and Rob.

—BUCHAN—
Land of Plenty

ROBERT SMITH

JOHN DONALD PUBLISHERS LTD
EDINBURGH

ISBN 0 85976 441 9

British Library Cataloguing in Publication Data
A catalogue record for this book is available from the British Library.

THE SCOTTISH ARTS COUNCIL

The publisher acknowledges subsidy from the Scottish Arts Council
towards the publication of this volume.

Typeset by
Pioneer Associates (Graphic) Ltd, Perthshire
Printed in Great Britain by
Bell & Bain Ltd., Glasgow

Acknowledgements

I am grateful to General Sir David Fraser for permission to quote from *The Christian Watt Papers*, and to the Leisure and Recreation Department of Banff and District Council for allowing me to quote a passage from Christian Watt Marshall's *A Stranger on the Bars*: to David Toulmin for permission to reproduce material from his *Collected Short Stories*, published by Gordon Wright Publishing Ltd; to Sacha Carnegie and William Heinemann Ltd for the extract from *Pigs I have Known*; and to Mrs J. Frolech, of Winterthur in Switzerland, for providing me with William Thomson's memoirs of his schooldays in Buchan.

For assistance with photographic material I have to thank Andrew Hill, Principal Curator, Aberdeenshire Heritage; Willie Milne, Assistant Curator, Aberdeenshire Farming Museum, and Mrs Lily Keith of Aberdeen, for both information and photographs.

Invaluable assistance was also given to me by the North East Scotland Library Service at Oldmeldrum and by the Local History Department of Aberdeen Central Library. I am also indebted to Kitty Reid, of Tarves, who gave so willingly of her time, and to many other people who dipped into their store of memories for me.

Finally, a word of thanks to my wife Sheila, who travelled with me through the Land of Plenty.

Aberdeen, 1996   Robert Smith

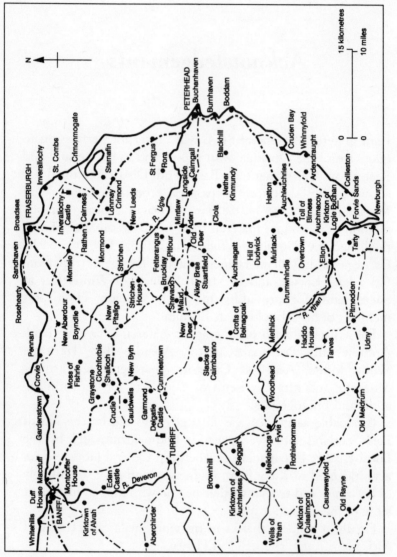

Location map

Contents

Introduction

Two centuries ago Buchan was known as the Land of Cakes, the granary of Scotland. In more recent times, the poet John C. Milne dubbed it the Land of Plenty – a place of 'peat-bogs and puddock-steels, weet and clorty widder'. This was the land that the Rev. Dr John B. Pratt made his own in his book, *Buchan*, published in 1858. It ran through five editions.

John Pratt's classic work was my principal guide as I wandered through Buchan discovering – or rediscovering – *The Land of Plenty*. At times it was, perhaps, too weighty a companion, too preoccupied with the lairds and their grand mansions, too little with the squalid homes of the crofters and farm workers, yet it was magnificent in its historical sweep, and always it served as a reminder that even in bleak and treeless Buchan there were 'wild ravines and rambling water-courses, verdant knolls and deep and tangled dells'.

In many ways, John Pratt led me to write this book. Even more important, however, was the fact that my roots were in Buchan. If my father hadn't left his job on a farm in Cruden to become a 'bobby' in Aberdeen, and if my mother hadn't given up her kitchie-deem's job at Tarty to put on a 'skivvy's' apron in the city, I might have ended up hyowin' neeps in Cruden. In fact, I had a taste of that back-breaking job when I was a lad.

I have always been proud of my background; relatives of mine seem to have farmed in almost every corner of Buchan. But I'm not alone in this. In his book, *Farm life in North-east Scotland*, Ian Carter said that if you found yourself in the company of an Aberdeen lawyer or surgeon and had difficulty in finding something to talk about the best thing to do was to turn the conversation to the social history of agriculture. 'All of these urbane, sophisticated men seem to have had an auntie in Echt or a cousin in New Pitsligo', he wrote. 'Aberdeen is a very rural city; its inhabitants' links with the surrounding countryside are deep and abiding'. Despite oil, that is still true to-day.

The Buchan borders tend to be elastic in this book; after all, even Dr Pratt seemed a little uncertain about them. At anyrate, bureaucracy has drawn Banff and Buchan together in recent years, which is reason enough for stretching them across the Deveron. In the same way, the old division of Formartine, which lay between the Don and Ythan, is now generally regarded as part of Buchan.

From time to time there have been suggestions that Pratt's *Buchan,* should be updated or completely revised and Flora Garry thought that someone should follow in Pratt's footsteps. This is neither a revision nor an update, but it does follow in the footsteps of Buchan's historian. John Pratt showed me the way and I took it . . . down to the Ythan estuary and its golden sands, north to Cruden where my father had worked the land, over the Waggle to the 'new towns' and into the castles and mansions of Buchan, along a muddy farm track to Lewis Grassic Gibbon's birthplace, up the Causeways of Kininmonth to the coast, across the windy braes of Clochforbie, and west by the Meer Road to Delgatie and the Deveron.

It is one man's view of the Land of Plenty . . . its towns, its farms and crofts, its culture, its humour, its struggle to retain its uniqueness. I like to think it follows the injunction of another poet, George Bruce, who came from Fraserburgh fisher stock. 'Let us praise them', he said of Buchan folk. 'They have made the land good'.

CHAPTER ONE

The Road to Tarty

The road to Tarty is a back door into Buchan. It chases the Tarty Burn to the mouth of the River Ythan, where another narrow road goes north to the kirkton of Logie-Buchan. Here, where the river puffs itself up like a monstrous serpent as it makes its last push towards the sea, great skeins of geese fill the sky and Arctic terns swoop over the Sands of Forvie.

Tarty is a flat, uncompromising landscape, always carrying a hint of the 'weet and clorty widder' that the Buchan poet J. C. Milne wrote about. It sits on the edge of a stretch of oozy mudflats known as the Sleeks of Tarty (the word 'sleek' means mire or mud), and its windy acres are broken only by a handful of farms. It was on a farm in Tarty that my mother spent part of her youth.

There was a ford and ferry at Tarty at one time and before the Waterside bridge was built there was another below the Sleeks, where carts would squelch their way over the mudflats at low tide and make their way to Waterside and through the Forvie Sands to Collieston. Other ferries operated on the river, the most important being the Boat of Logie, which was on the main route to the north.

From the farm of Meikle Tarty I walked down a rough track to where the Sleeks' muddy fingers reached out into the estuary. Half-way across the river the mudflats wrap themselves around an island called Inch Geck, which covers an area of three acres. The grass on Inch Geck was once said to be good for fattening cattle. Certainly, the birds seem to find food on the island, for great flocks of them were hovering over it when I was there. 'Inch' means island and 'Geck' is the Scots word for fool, and, oddly enough, Jamie Fleeman, the

1

Laird of Udny's Fool, lived at Knockhall Castle, which looks down on Inch Geck.

Fleeman saved the Knockhall family from death when the castle was accidentally burned to the ground in 1734, but he had no great desire to save the cook, who perpetually tormented him with her cry of 'Peats, peats, Fleeman!' and 'Water, water, Fleeman!' In the end, when the fire was at her bedroom door, he relented and went up the smoke-filled stairs and woke her, crying, 'Come awa', ye jade, or ye'll get twa het hurdies!' — two hot buttocks.

The Howe of Tarty lies at the foot of the track which runs down from Meikle Tarty to the estuary, and it was there, at the curiously-numbered '2 Howe of Tarty', within a stone's throw of the river, that I met a young Australian, Dave Skidmore, and his wife, Tina, a nurse, who had come to live on the banks of the Ythan. Dave worked on the oil rigs, but with the big boom over and oil companies shedding jobs he was 'on the beach', awaiting a call that would take him off-shore again. All day long he would hear the clatter of helicopters flying over the estuary on their way to the North Sea oil fields. He took me indoors to meet a new member of the family, Jamie, who had been born only five days earlier. Tarty had acquired another resident — and little Jamie could claim to be a Buchan loon with Aussie blood in him.

That first winter they faced blizzard conditions at Tarty, with frost and snow throwing an icy coat over the Ythan estuary. Their water pipes froze, broke up, and had to be replaced, but none of this blunted their enthusiasm for their new home in the Howe. The simple fact was that Dave and Tina had given their hearts to Tarty, loving its isolation, its dune-skirted river, and its sense of tranquillity. It is not surprising, for the mouth of the Ythan can at times be hauntingly beautiful.

It sometimes seems as if the whole estuary has become a vast bird sanctuary. You look up and swans are flying over her head, their great wings beating the air as their long, elegant necks point the way across the river. Away to the north, as dusk creeps in, the sky is darkened by migrant geese dropping down on the Meikle Loch, which is half a mile long and lies behind the Kippie Hills. At dawn, ducks rise in a flurry of wings, their peace disturbed by the sound of guns, Dave told me that they were often wakened at five o'clock in the morning by wildfowlers out duck-shooting.

The tinkers came to this back-o'-beyond corner in the old days. Flora Garry wrote about them in 'Spring Fever', a poem about how the changing seasons had stirred their gypsy blood and taken them away from the 'cassey steens' of Aberdeen, north by the Buchan road. In a sense I was following the tinkers' trail . . . 'throwe Cloverhill and Tarbot hill, by Blairton's cottar raw' and on to 'the braes o' Logie'.

I could imagine their 'cairts' rattling down the road to the Ythan, with the tinks' minds on 'besoms, caups an pins an sowderin fiteiron', and 'a smarrach o barfit geets!' hanging from the float. But they never stayed long at Tarty, for their thoughts were on their summer quarters on a hill at Tyrie —

So they'll nae deval by Tarty's waal,
Nor daachle lang at Udny,
The hedder hulls afore them lie,
Their simmer hame Turlundie.

Down at the Sleeks the riverbank curves away to a spit of land known as the Snub (pronounced Snob), a favourite fishing spot, where swans are often seen sailing majestically down-river. The abundance of food that this corner of the estuary provides makes it a haunt of wildfowl. At one time it attracted a greater variety of water birds and sea fowl than any other river on the east coast of Scotland. In 1885, a long list of birds on the Ythan included both the northern and red-throated diver, the black-billed auk, the greenheaded goosander and the solan goose.

A century later, many of the same species still come to the Ythan estuary and at the Cultery Field Centre in Newburgh, run by Aberdeen University's zoology department, scientists are putting all this bird life under the microscope. They have laboratories and lecture rooms at Cultery, but much of their work is done on the estuary and across the river on the Sands of Forvie Nature Reserve, which has the largest concentration of eider duck in Britain. Colonies of terns breed among the sand dunes near the mouth of the river. The field station at Cultery was originally a private bird sanctuary and two ponds at the centre are still used by straying migrants.

The Forvie Sands were likened by one 19th-century writer to 'the deserts of Zahara', and when you walk across them and the seas of sand swallow you up it is hard to believe that this 2000-acre wilderness, with a 'lost' village buried under it, is within sight of Newburgh.

From the links at Newburgh I looked across the estuary to Forvie. I could hear the distant growling of the sea. It made me think of a small boy who had cocked his ear to the same sound nearly a century ago. Not long after moving into a tenement in the village, he looked through a gap in the sand dunes and caught his first glimpse of the sea . . . 'flat, crouching and angry, thrashing itself on the sand to the edge of the world. Its steady, muttering groan was the background of sound against the silence in which we all lived'.

That four-year-old boy was James McBey, who was to become one of the finest British etchers of this century. He was born in a blacksmith's cottage a mile south of Newburgh. He shivered in this bleak corner of Buchan and came to the conclusion that it was 'inhabited by survivors'. His ambition to become an artist was first fired when he entered a competition for a drawing of Knockhall Castle. It was the only entry, but it won him a prize of 2s 6d.

In his autobiography, *The Early Life of James McBey*, he described Newburgh as a village of austere blue-slated houses where half the population made a livelihood off the other half. But time has changed the face of the village; modern houses line its main street, many of them occupied by oil workers. The Australian, Dave Skidmore, lived in Newburgh for a time and became part of the 'oil' community there.

Some things, however, haven't changed. The nine-hole golf

4

course on the Udny Links, where young McBey hit a lacerated gutta-perch golf ball with a cleek, is still there, and the ancient graveyard on the Inches, a finger of land jutting out into the estuary, is a link with the days of Alexander III and the Comyn Earl of Buchan, who founded a pre-Reformation chapel known as the Red Chapel of Buchan. The Udny family burial vault is in the graveyard, where the winds off the river sing a dirge around its faded tombstones. Beyond the Inches are Mitchell and Rae's grain warehouses, now converted to other uses, which once dominated the approach to the village from the north.

The Ythan estuary and its mudflats, and the boats that plied up and down the river, fascinated James McBey. Back in 1648, two centuries before McBey was born, the mouth of the Ythan was said to be obstructed by a moveable sand bar and the river was 'only navigable for small craft'. Nearly a century and a half later the 1793 Statistical Account reported that Newburgh had only one fishing boat, 'chiefly used for piloting vessels up the river'. When McBey was a lad, two small steam boats and one sailing vessel operated on the Ythan. Local fishermen acted as pilots, making it their business to know the treacherous, shifting bar, which was 'altered by every gale'.

It is hard to believe that any ships were able to sail up the Ythan, for, although it is the biggest estuary in Aberdeenshire, some stretches of it almost seem hard put to rival the Tarty Burn, Swollen by the tide, it fills a basin 700 yards wide, but upstream its spindly body is too thin and delicate for its head. It was once called 'a shrunken giant', yet this was the river that sustained Newburgh as a busy port for many years. It even had a Newburgh Shipmasters' Friendly Society.

Dr John Pratt watched punts being propelled up the river by a pole or 'set' eighteen or twenty feet long, but behind them as the years passed came flat-bottomed lighters, puffing up the river to the Meadows at Waterton, a quarter of a mile below Ellon, and down on the estuary schooner's and steam vessels sailed in to export grain from Mitchell and Rae's warehouses and import coal, timber and bones. In 1841, a 300-feet-long wharf was built to accommodate vessels trading to the 'Creek'. It was still being used by a lone cargo vessel in the 1970s.

The only other boats on the Ythan were the ferry boats. There were two at the Boat of Logie, one a small boat used for day-to-day ferrying, the other a large boat acting as a 'Sunday Special' for kirkgoers crossing the river from the north side to Logie-Buchan Church on the south side.

Logie-Buchan is linked to Tarty to-day by a narrow back-road running north from Meikle Tarty to the kirkton. The folk there had to wait until 1932 for their bridge and what they got was a curious hump-backed structure built to commemorate its war dead. The bridge was given its enormous hump so that vessels could pass underneath it, but now it seems laughably out-of-date, an eccentric piece of bridge-building on a river with no traffic except rafts taking part in an annual raft race. On the other hand, it adds a little character to a lovely stretch of the river and it helps to keep the world away from Logie-Buchan, which is no bad thing.

You climb on to the old bridge's hump and watch the Ythan waters swirl lazily downstream to Newburgh, thinking about the river's long journey from the Wells of Ythan, through the Howe of Auchterless to Towie, past Fyvie and the brooding Braes o' Gight to Haddo, and on to Tarty and the sand dunes of Forvie. It is still and quiet here, but it wasn't always so. In the 17th century markets were held at the church, which so upset the 'unco-good' that the Presbytery had to stop them being held on the Lord's Day. Not only that, they also had to put a ban on wrestling matches and football on the Sabath.

The kirk and its manse are on the south side of the bridge. It was from there, seventy-five years ago, that the Rev. James Coutts, minister of Logie-Buchan, set out for the Station Buffet at Ellon to marry a domestic servant, Elizabeth Hutcheon Murdoch, and a police constable, Andrew Smith. John

Murdoch, a farm grieve in Tarty, gave the bride away. He was my grandfather and the newly-weds were my parents.

The new bridge had yet to be built, so the Rev. Mr Coutts either went to Ellon by the Meikle Tarty road or crossed the Ythan by ferry. The cottage on the north side carries the name 'Ferryboat' on its gate and the road running past it leads to the junction at Denhead, where signs point to Auchmacoy, Ellon and Collieston.

The tiny community of Auchmacoy is full of surprises. It boasts a magnificent hall with stained glass windows and a Tudor-type house attached to it. 'Naebody uses it now', a local told me. 'Just the Rurals'. On the grass in front of it is a salmon cobble, permanently grounded, well away from the river and now, filled with earth, acting as a flower bed. Here, too, in the Land of Neeps and Tatties, you sniff the air for a scent of more exotic fare — a taste of goulash, perhaps, seasoned with paprika — for the Ellon side of the junction a sign says 'Hungarian Restaurant and Cafe'. Jan Wadovsky was an oil worker for twelve years, became redundant, and decided to tempt Buchan with such alien dishes.

Meanwhile, down on the Ythan, the waters ripple over centuries of history. The ferryman — the 'Boaties' — have their place in it, for they were once kings of the river. The ferries were usually operated by members of one family. Four generations of Barracks, starting with John Barak in 1631, served as ferryman at Kinharrachie until the late 18th century. One was recorded as being 'at the Bott'. The Kinharrachie boatman was a William Crighton, who ferried himself into the 20th century as 'Auld Boatie'.

The steam tugs that paddled up the Ythan from Newburgh unloaded their cargoes at the Meadows, a mile from the bridge at Ellon. Mitchell and Rae had their grain warehouse there. The ruins of the ancient Castle of Waterton, a seat of the Forbeses, are near here on the north bank. James Fleeman was often seen at Waterton and when I was walking by the river I met a man who told me a story about the Laird of

7

Waterton and the Laird of Udny's Fool. He came striding down the path to the Meadows, a big, bearded giant of a man who looked as if he had been born to his job, for he was water bailiff on the Ythan.

Alistair McCurrach had been a bailiff for fifty years. He was at one time a bailiff at Newburgh and he knew the river and its folk like the back of his hand. Many a tale he could tell about them. He would have got on fine with Jamie Fleeman, for he has always liked Jamie's pin-sharp humour, and he particularly admires the way Fleeman stood up to his so-called betters. He thinks Buchan folk have been shabby in their treatment of the Laird o' Udny's Fool and he believes that more should be done to make his story known.

The burly bailiff has a fondness for the tale of how Jamie was lying on the banks of the Ythan near the Meadows, basking in the sun, when he was hailed from the other side of the water by the Laird of Waterton, who was on horseback and wanted to know the best place to ford the river. Jamie, who had no great affection for the Laird, directed him to the deepest pool in the river and then watched him sink up to his neck in water.

When he struggled, half-drowned, on the bank he turned on Fleeman and angrily accused him of trying to drown him.

'Gosh be here, laird', said Fleeman, 'I've seen the geese and dukes crossin' there hunners o' times an' I'm sure your horse has langer legs than ony o' them'.

It was the last day of the salmon season when I followed the path to Ellon. The river seemed to be choked with fishers. I watched two of them hauling in a pair of fair-sized fish. Not long before that I had been talking to Alastair McCurrach about the time when people probed the Ythan waters for a much greater 'catch' — pearls. Pearl fishing was a recognised industry in Buchan, running all through the summer, but it began to die out at the beginning of this century. 'There are very few regulars pearlers', reported The Book of Buchan in 1910, 'and, in fact, the business is now practically in the hands of vagrants'.

From where I was walking I could see the busy road above and the local cemetery, where my grandfather was buried. I left the riverbank and went in search of my roots.

CHAPTER TWO
The Karny Wynke

The old croft of Auchleuchries lies five miles north of Ellon, beyond the Toll of Birness and only a short distance from the Halfway House, where the road runs on to Mintlaw and Fraserburgh. The cottar house that stood on the croft has long since gone, replaced by a modern bungalow. It has always seemed to me to be out of place, an alien building. Every time I pass it I think of the house that was once there, with its cold flagstone floor and a box bed in the wall where old John Murdoch, my grandfather, slept.

Old Jock's dark, bearded face lingers in my memory. He lived out his days at Auchleuchries, with his housekeeper, Bathie, to look after him, and whatever else he did in his long life he made sure that the name of Murdoch was handed down to future generations. He fathered sixteen sons and daughters, which was notable even in an age when big families were commonplace. I was once told that I had forty-nine cousins, and that was only on my mother's side.

The sad result of all this was that my grandmother died at the age of forty-six, leaving my mother — the eldest daughter — to look after the family. In time, Jock's brood grew up and was scattered like chaff to farms all over Buchan, some later emigrating to Canada, others drifting to the towns to join the police. My father, who was a fee'd loon at Chanonry Knap in Cruden, took this escape route, like the lad in 'Nicky Tams'.

I've often thought I'd like tae be
A bobby on the force,
Or maybe I'll get on the trams
Tae drive a pair o'horse.

When I stayed at my grandfather's croft as a boy I thought there was only one Auchleuchries. I had no interest in what lay beyond. I didn't know that there were other farms in the area called Auchleuchries, or that there was a Moss of Auchleuchries and a Hill of Auchleuchries (a poor lump of a thing, as it turned out), and I had no idea that there had been an Auchleuchries Castle, although it was once described as nothing more than 'a mansion house dignified by a square tower'.

Nor did anybody tell me about the soldier of fortune from Easter Auchleuchries, who had a name that was half-Scots and half-Russian — Patrick Ivanovitsch, better known in Buchan as Patrick Gordon. A son of John Gordon of Auchleuchries, Patrick was born in 1635, left home at the age of sixteen to take up a military career, and ended up as a General in the Russian Army.

He was a close friend of Peter the Great, who wept at his bedside when he died in November, 1699. Lord Byron wrote a mocking verse about Patrick Ivanovitsch and his Russian masters:

Then you've General Gordon,
Who girded his sword on,
To serve with a Muscovite master,
And help him to polish
A nation so owlish
They thought shaving their beards
    a disaster.

Only a fence separated my grandfather's croft from Easter Auchleuchries, where Patrick Gordon was born. I have some-times wondered if Old Jock had ever heard of him and his Muscovite masters. He would certainly have had a fellow-feeling for the Russians and their beards, for he was proud of his own whiskers.

The countryside north of the Ythan throws up the names

of many places that the General knew and visited when he came home on leave. Most of them were Gordon seats lying by the Ebrie burn, which rises below New Deer and wriggles its way south almost on a line with the old Buchan railway. There are other names that are not on any maps and are long forgotten; the 'Bony Wyfe's' on the Blackhill of Dudwick, for instance, and the Karny Wynke. 'I rose up early,' wrote Patrick Gordon, 'and walked up to the Kairne and to the Karny Wynke'.

I followed the General's footsteps to Ebriehead, passing Nethermuir, which was once said to be 'about a bleak a spot as any in Buchan', and from there I went east to Crichie, where four hills stand guard over Stuartfield. They are diminutive peaks even by comparison with little Mormond, but Crichie folk are apt to look at you askance if you mock them. The late Cuthbert Graham wrote a poem about them:

> The 'island' o' Crichie's a braw little toon,
> Though Stuartfield by rights is the name o' the place,
> Wi' four famous hills that stand guardian a' roon
>   Ca'ad Scroghill an' Jock,
>   West Crichie an' Knock,
> An' its aye been the hame o' a long-livin' race.

Stuartfield, which was laid out on the Crichie estate in 1772 and named after Captain John Stuart, a warrior of Marlborough's campaigns, is still called Crichie by some older people. The village is in a different mould from many other 'new towns'. Back at the end of last century one of its streets, West Street, was known as Little Hell Street because of the fights between local youths and tinkers. Blood and hair flew all over the place, according to one report.

It had more odd characters than half a dozen of the 'new towns' put together, worthies like the Royals, who were said to live like rabbits in a warren, or 'Hunchback Sammy' and a 'decrepit wee mannie' called Willie Bamilton ('Oh, Willie Bamilton!' they sang, 'You can hear the ladies cry . . .'), and

Old Angus, a cobbler, who made boots as tough as toffee and toffee as tough as boots.

Old Angus's living room served both as a workshop and a sweetie factory. It was there that he mended tackety boots and made treacle candy as a sideline. The candy was boiled and hung on a hook on the back of the door, where Angus teased it with his hands until it turned a rich golden colour. It was sticky work and he spat liberally on his hands to keep the candy from adhering to them. When it was ready he took his cobbling hammer and knife and broke it into ha'penny portions.

Times change and the old ways are slipping away from the folk of Crichie, but the village pump still stands defiantly in the Square, a place where old-timers are apt to meet and talk about the good old days. As Bert Graham put it:

> The Pump in the Square
> Is still happily there,
> Where cronies can meet for
>   a gossip or claik.

If Stuartfield had a coat-of-arms its heraldic symbols would have to be the village pump and the village bell. The village bell was to Stuartfield what the townhouse clock is to Aberdeen. It stood not far from the pump and was rung at nine o'clock in the morning, at one o'clock in the afternoon, and at eight o'clock in the evening, curfew time. That was in the days when local schoolchildren acted as herds to feuars' cattle grazing on the village Commonty.

The village bell hasn't rung out for eighty-five years — it was taken down in 1911. It was a Heath Robinson affair, with a pole and a spidery frame reaching up to the sky and the bell at its apex. I would like to see the folk of Crichie build another village bell. They could raise it beside the village pump and let it ring out on special occasions. They might even find a latter-day Old Angus who would turn his hand to a spot of candy-making.

The Knock of the four-hills poem gives its name to a hand-ful of farms. One of them is half a mile east of Stuartfield on the Longside road. Here, what must be a unique record of continuous farming tenure was established, with five genera-tions of the Keith family tilling the land of Wester Knock for over 200 years.

The first was George Keith, who in 1759 rented Wester Knock from the Cumines of Kininmonth at £60 Scots. The last was his great-great-great-grandson, William Keith, who gave up a banking/business career to take over the farm in 1963. He died in November, 1978 . . . it was the end of the Keith saga.

Bill Keith's widow, Lily, kept the farm going for another couple of years, but finally sold it. A former teacher in Buchan, she has carried out considerable research into the Keith family and the history of Crichie. The year 1782 stands out: it was known as the Year of the Bad Hairst, when a great snowstorm swept over Buchan. It was also the year in which the first William Keith was born. When he was a young boy his mother told him about it . . . about how the storm came when the corn was still uncut, about how she took a hot drink to the shearers in the field, carrying her bairn with her, and about how it was 'such a day of smore drift' that she was afraid that the child would be smothered before they reached the house.

They got home safely, but next day all the stooks were completely covered in snow and most of the cereal crops were destroyed. Because of this disaster the laird, John Burnett, who founded the village, gave 'discharge in full' to James Keith in Wester Knock for 19 bolls, being half of the oat crop of '82.

Lily told me, too, of how she heard about the great days of Aikey Fair, when a stream of horses began to arrive early on the morning of the Fair. There were hundreds of them, some in bunches of twenty to fifty, each one tied to the other's tail, and only two or three men in charge of them. Then there were the days when the farmers and their families went to kirk

14

on Sunday morning – or had a very good reason for not going. Gig after gig drove down through the village to the parish church or the Episcopal church in Old Deer, or to the Free kirk at the end of the dysters' dam.

Following the old practice of giving the farm's name (Wastie for Wester) to the farmer, Bill Keith's grandfather was known as Aul' Wastie and his son was called Wastie. There is a tale told about how, when Aul' Wastie was courting a teacher at Rora School, he turned up at the school and declared that he was the Inspector of Schools. He spoke to the youngsters, looked at their work, and announced that because they were so good they could all have a half-day. The school was 'skailed', the pupils scurried off home – and away went 'Wastie' with his girl-friend.

The north end of Stuartfield is known as Quartalehouse. Although there was an alehouse in the village at one time, the name has no connection with it. It is said to come from the Gaelic Gort-lie-mor, which means 'the field between two streams'. I imagine this was why Bert Graham wrote about the 'island' of Crichie.

Before I left the village I went up Knock Hill to get a bird's-eye view of the 'island of Crichie'. I could see the Knock road rolling down through the village and climbing away to Windhill, which isn't regarded as one of Stuartfield's 'guardian' tops. I was looking for kirk steeples. There were five kirks in Stuartfield at one time (our Buchan historian, John Pratt, was curate at the Episcopal church from 1821 to 1825), but today there is none.

I could see the road to Old Deer, which was less than a mile to the north, but I was going south to other hills, to Dudwick and Muirtack and the Hill of Auchleuchries. Although it lay near one of the main highways through Buchan, the road I took seemed remote from the outside world. There was a curious sense of isolation about it . . . a feeling of great space and solitude, and across the bare, flat acres of Buchan the views seemed to sweep away, wide and limitless, to unreachable horizons. Here and there ruined crofts scarred the landscape and narrow roads spawned even narrower tracks leading to holdings with names like Toddlehills, Clamandwells, Skelmuir and Humblecairn.

There was also a proliferation of Backhills — Backhill of Coldwells, Backhill of Fortrie, Backhill of Dudwick — which in a district where the hills struggle to reach a height of 500ft, seemed inappropriate. But there are two theories about the name. One is that it means an unploughed ridge, the other that it comes from *bac*, a moss. So here again was a reminder of how farms and crofts were wrestled from Buchan's peat bogs.

Five miles north of Ellon, where a sliver of road goes cavorting up and down the map as if drawn by a drunken cartographer, the Hill of Dudwick rises to a height of 571ft, making it the highest point in the district. This was where Patrick Gordon had 'a standing drink' at the 'Bony Wyfe's'. The Aberdeen Sasines of 1686 described Bonnywife's as a croft, but by the early 18th century there was no trace of it in the records.

So who *was* the Bonny Wife? Up on the Hill of Dudwick I found myself imagining her as a plump, sonsy lass, hurrying from her croft to hand up a stirrup cup to the great General who had come riding up to her door on that bleak and windy hill in Buchan two centuries ago. Where the croft had been I never discovered, and as I went on my way I was thinking about another mysterious spot mentioned in Gordon's Diary — the Karny Wynke. 'Kairny' or Cairny simply means a heap, of stones. A wink or winnock is old Scots for a window, and it may be that it was the window of a drinking howff, which many cottar houses were, and that Patrick had strolled up from Westerton, which was farmed by his brother John, to quench his thirst.

Going over the Hill of Auchleuchries, I stopped at a roadside cottage half-hidden by trees and bushes. It was a desolate, depressing place, its crumbling walls buried under a mass of ivy, and it was difficult to imagine that anyone had lived there. In a field on the other side of the road was a stone building with a red corrugated roof; a byre, I thought, for cattle were grazing in the sparse grass around it.

It was there that I met Alex Bruce, from Ellon, who had come up the hill from the direction of the Halfway House. He told me that he had once lived at Hillhead of Auchleuchries and added, to my surprise, that his father had worked the Croft of Cairnywink. Taken aback by this coincidence, I asked where it was. He pointed across the fence to the building in the field. 'That's it', he said. It was all that was left of General Gordon's 'Karny Wynke'.

At one time it had been occupied by a souter, while the ruined cottage on the other side of the road had been a tailor's shop. As for the 'Karne', it was farther down the hill, a cairn built into a dyke about half a mile from the Ellon road on Westerton Farm.

Not far from Cairnywink is the farm of Muirtack, where I unearthed some more information. I had been searching for someone who remembered my grandfather, or who had heard about him, but I had little success. 'Try the Adamsons of Muirtack', I was told. 'They've been in the area longest'. Muirtack of Auchleuchries is mentioned several times in General Gordon's Diary, mostly in connection with land charters. In 1670, for instance, John Gordon of Auchleuchries sold to his son, 'Collonel Patrick Gordon, and the now deceast Catharin Vanbuckowen,* then his spowse, the lands of Achluchries, Easter and Wester, with the pendicles thereof, called Murstack, the Milne of Auchleuchries, milne lands, multures, and sequelles'.

Pendicles are out-farms, areas of land which are subsidiary to larger estates. 'Muir tacks' were 'tenancies of hilly land as distinguished from more improved land'. The description still stands, for Muirtack lies on the north side of the Hill of Auchleuchries, looking across to the Moss of Auchleuchries. Most of the moss has been reclaimed, but a hint of what it was

---

*Katharine von Bockhoven, daughter of Philip von Bockhoven, was 'scarcely thirteen' when she married Patrick Gordon.

once like can be found in a distant red-roofed building which Alex Bruce pointed out to me. It was called Piggerbog.

When I went in search of Muirtack I was told to look out for 'an old farm', and that was what it was, an old-fashioned farm with no frills, just glaur and sharn and provocative smells — and arrogant peacocks strutting about the yard. There was a midden on its doorstep and a mountain of dung, and behind it was the byre, with its half-doors, its wooden stalls, and cattle shuffling about in their own mess. Charlie Adamson, taking me through the byre to the neep shed, said it was a lot of work looking after them. He believes in the old ways. Until a few years ago he was still doing his harvesting with a binder.

Three bachelors live at Muirtack. Two of them, Charlie and his brother Willie, were there when I arrived, and with them was Joe Chessor, who farmed at Auquharney, near Hatton, until he retired. Now he has his home at the Castlepark housing estate in Ellon. They were 'newsin' about the old days. Charlie's memory goes a long way back. He has been at Muirtack for sixty years, which was round about the time I was a loon climbing my grandfather's ricks at Auchleuchries. He couldn't remember the old man.

Joe and Wullie thought that it would have been a 6-acre croft. Back in the 1930s the average size of a croft was about 10 acres. Joe concluded that there would probably have been 'twa coos and twa pigs' at Auchleuchries — most crofts that size had them. I could remember twa coos, but no pigs.

The tailor on the Hill of Auchleuchries sold clothes and sweeties and other household goods. Charlie got *his* sweeties there; it was surprising, he said, how much you could get for a penny in those days. Digging into his pocket, he produced a handful of old pennies, one so thin you could barely read the writing on it. He had found them down at the ruined tailor's shop and thought you could find a lot more if you had a metal detector.

'You don't need a metal detector', said Joe. 'I'll show you

what you need'. He rose, went out to his car, and came back with a dowsing rod in his hand. He had used it to find water and to check on choked drains when farming at Auquharney, and now he showed what it could do picking out 20p coins on Charlie's carpet. He let me try it out and it worked, much to my surprise. It was true what they said; there was nothing to beat the old ways of doing things.

The old-timers knew about Cairnywink, but nobody knew who built the cairn at the dyke, or why. It was said to be a boundary marker, but Joe thought it was more like an early direction post. 'We hae General Gordon tae harp on aboot', said a leaflet put out by the Central Buchan Tourism Group, who claimed that the Cairn had been erected in memory of Patrick Gordon, but there was nothing on it to say so. Joe thought that too many people were harpin' on aboot the Gordons, so I left them to it. Before I said farewell to Muirtack, Charlie took me out to the neep shed and, telling me to hold out my hands, dropped a monster turnip on to them. It almost brought me to my knees. 'Ye'll need tae tak' an aixe till't', he said.

Patrick Gordon had always planned to come home to Scotland to spend his last years in Buchan, having given over all rights to the lands of Auchleuchries to his eldest son John, while at the same time making provision for himself and his second wife, Elizabeth Born Roonaer. He laid down that he and his wife should be paid three hundred Scottish merks yearly and 'be infeft in the lands of two pleughs of Easter Auchluchries'. In other words, they were to be given as much land as two pleughs could till on Easter Auchleuchries, where he was born.

But Patrick doubted that he would ever return to Buchan. 'It is a dangerous time now', he wrote to the Earl of Aberdeen in 1682, 'and the old proverb proveth but too oft true':

Non pater a filio, non hospote tutus,
Non socer a genero, fratrum quoque gratia rara est.

He died on 29 November, 1699. The man who had left Buchan as 'a poor unfriended wanderer' had his eyes closed by the hands of an Emperor. Before he died he cleared his estate of debt, but after his death 'the cloud of wadsets (mortgages) soon began to thicken again'. Thirty years later, Easter Auchleuchries passed to another race of Gordons when it was purchased by Alexander Gordon of Sandend.

It was to Easter Auchleuchries that I went at the end of my travels around this Gordon land . . . to my grandfather's croft. The farm road leading to it is just past the Half-way House, and as I was walking up to it I was seeing in my mind, not the white-walled building that stands there now, but the old cottar house. I passed the space near the house where Old Jock had built his two ricks, and the field running down to the burn where he had grazed his two cows.

There was nothing there that I recognised. Steve Foster, who worked in Fraserburgh, and his wife Kath had been in the house for a year. They liked it — they had five bedrooms. Grandfather Murdoch had a box-bed with doors that closed and shut out the world. He had a big open fire with pots bubbling on the swey. He had a porch with hens clucking about the doorway and a steading behind the house. But all that was a long time ago — now the past had been wiped out.

CHAPTER THREE

Souters of Cruden

Fed by streams from the Moss of Auchleuchries and the Bog of Ardallie, the Water of Cruden comes tumbling out of the hills not far from where my grandfather had his croft near Easterton of Auchleuchries. It runs from there to Hatton, swinging round the curiously-named Aad Braes and sweeping into the sea at 'the waird of Crudane'.

That was the name of the tiny fishing community at the mouth of the Cruden burn three centuries ago, but times change and names change with them. 'The Ward' gave way to Port Erroll, and in 1924 the village, originally known as Invercruden, was re-named Cruden Bay.

Dr John Pratt thought that the Water of Cruden was 'a sadly harassed brook' because in its eight-mile journey to the sea it had to turn the wheels of seven mills. It has a special place in my affections, for it is a stream that travels where my roots are strongest . . . at the farm of Chanonry Knap, where my grandfather was a tenant farmer, at Cruden Bay itself and down in the old kirkyard by the Bishop's Bridge, on the road to Hatton and along the coast to Whinnyfold, where the sea winds make a blustery landfall on a clutter of clifftop cottages.

It was to Whinnyfold that I went to learn about my links with Buchan, not about my family tree (I had left that too late, as often happens) but about the land – my land – and its people. I discovered that the Buchan tongue can often make a nonsense of its place-names. My father always spoke about Finnyfa', and when he said 'Chanonry Knap' he ran the words together so that they sounded like Shanricknap. When I became aware of the real pronunciation I assumed that the word 'Chanonry' had a religious origin, as in *chanry-kirk*,

21

which was near enough to 'Shanriknap', but, in fact, it comes from an old Scots word *channery*, meaning gravelly. So my father had been a fee'd loon on a gravelly, lumpy little hill (or *knap*) on the road to Cruden Bay.

Not long before his death in December, 1987, R. F. Mackenzie, an Aberdeen headmaster who was sacked for his progressive views on education, wrote a book called *A Search for Scotland*. In it, he told how his mother came from Whinnyfold, which Mackenzie likened to another clifftop community, Catterline. His book carried a cover picture of Joan Eardley's painting of the Mearns village. I had an aunt who lived in Finnyfa', but I never met her, for I knew little of my father's family. Mackenzie, on the other hand, was a frequent visitor to the village and would often go out fishing with his grand-uncle, who would take his yawl under the cliffs between Whinnyfold and Collieston, where the Spanish galleon, the *Santa Caterina*, is said to have sunk in 1588.

I was thinking of Mackenzie, this 'prophet without honour', when walking on the cliffs south of the village. He wrote about these 'fretted knife edges of granite rock', reminding me of how I had once climbed down them to photograph gulls breeding on the very edge of the sea ... 'a lonely, eerie place, alien to human beings', he called it. Guillemots and kittiwakes squawked over my head and I found, like the men in the yawl, that I was an unwelcome intruder. The drama of the Spanish Armada sent me back to Mackenzie's book when I was exploring what had happened on the Buchan coast after the sinking of the *Santa Caterina*, but there was another battle in my mind as I made my way down to the Bay of Cruden.

Up on the brae at the north end of Finnyfa' a path drops down to the shore, opening up a breathtaking view of the bay. Here, the jagged teeth of the Scaurs of Cruden reach out into the sea, waiting, like the jaws of some brooding sea monster, to devour unwary mariners. In another age, seamen might have had such superstitious thoughts, for the appetite of the Scaurs for stricken ships was insatiable.

From the Scaurs the beach swings round in a two-mile arc to the Water of Cruden, its sands, as Dr Pratt put it, 'as smooth and firm as the floor of a cathedral'. He was impressed by the scenery, 'exuberant with wild flowers', and he climbed up to Hawklaw, a headland in the centre of the bay, to look north to Buchanness lighthouse and south to the Bay of Aberdeen.

It was at Hawklaw in 1014 that the Danes and their Norwegian allies landed and fought their last bloody battle with the Scots. There was no Cruden Bay then, and the battle is said to have raged along 'a plain in the Bay of Arden-draught. The farm of Aulton of Ardendraught lies less than half a mile from the shore. 'Cruden' is supposed to have come from *Croju-Dane* or *Crudane*, the crushing or slaughter of the Danes; a fanciful thought, but that was what happened, although neither side, shattered by the bitter fighting, could claim a great victory.

The battle extended inland for four miles on the south side of the Water of Cruden, which meant that when I was playing war games on my grandfather's croft as a boy it was on ground where two mighty armies had fought each other to a standstill. Relics of the battle were found in the area, including a neck-chain and battle-axe on the Hill of Ardiffery. They say that the graves of the slain could be seen in the Howe of Ardendraught until early last century, when a farmer at Nethermill, who was more interested in bawbees than battles, decided to wipe out a slice of Buchan history with his plough.

The tide of battle would have washed over little Hobshill, a tiny 200-feet peak near Hatton. Hobshill overlooks Auquharney, where Joe Chessor farmed until his retirement. I met him at Charlie Adamson's farm at Muirtack, where we sat and yarned about the old days, about General Patrick Gordon, friend of the Tsar of Russia, and about all the other Gordons in Buchan. Joe, frowning a little, said he thought there were too many of them — 'they're a' ower the place'. It reminded me of Johnny Gibb of Gushetneuk and his cry of 'Bruce for

23

ever! Gordon never!' He couldn't understand why the
Gordons were all supposed to be giants of men, 6 feet, or
over. He had been to Haddo House and had seen the beds
there — and *they* looked about 4½ feet long. He couldn't
figure out how the Gordons slept. 'Like this?' said Charlie,
curling himself up in a ball. Joe wondered if they might have
been like the Danes, who were tall and slept in chairs with
their legs stretched out.

I never discovered how Joe had become an authority on
the Danes, or where he had learned about their long legs, but
later, when I was standing on Hawklaw, I remembered the
conversation at Muirtack. According to Pratt's *Buchan*, a
chapel was built on the spot where the Danish dead were
buried, but it was 'overlaid and drowned by the sands' in a
storm similar to the one that buried Forvie. Another was
erected in a more suitable place and here you could see 'the
huge and almost gigantic bones of those that fell in the battle
of Croju-Dane.

The *Chronicles of Scotland* also had something to say about
how a kirk was 'biggit', then another, 'with mair magnificence' and on a site 'mair ganand' (landward), and about the
giant warriors who died in the Bay of Ardendraught: 'Sindry
of their bonis was sene be us, mair like giandis than common
stature of men: throw quhilk apperis that men in auld times
hes bene of mair stature and quantite than ony men are
presently in our days'.

I had left Hawklaw half-expecting to see giants striding
about the links, descendants of the Danes who came roaring
ashore at Cruden in the 'auld times'. The Gordons weren't
the only people in Buchan with long legs. Early this century
the ranks of the Aberdeen police force were swollen by brawny
farm servants like my father. It could be said that Buchan
'bobbies' were 'mair like giandis than common stature of
men'. They were escaping from the dreary darg of life as a
first baillie or an orra loon, and in those days brawn was
more important than brain in upholding the law. Buchan
could supply plenty of that.

Many of the Danes and Norwegians were converted to Christianity and a lasting peace came out of the carnage at the Bay of Ardendraught. To-day, the bond remains firm. In July, 1914, exactly 900 years after the Battle of Cruden, Kommander Trygve Gran stood at the Kirk of Cruden and asked God's blessing on the first flight across the North Sea from Cruden Bay to Norway. Other flights followed and in the church, a model of Kommander Gran's plane, made by the pupils of Hatton and Port Erroll schools, hangs between the flags of Norway and Scotland. The coming of oil also forged closer links between the two countries and the land-fall of BP's North Sea oil pipeline from the Forties Field is on the golf course near Hawklaw.

I left Cruden Bay and followed the Water of Cruden towards Hatton. I was making for the Kirk of Cruden, which stands within a stone's throw of the Bishop's Bridge, a narrow picturesque one-arched bridge built in 1697 by Dr James Drummond, the Bishop of Brechin, who went to live at Slains Castle after being deprived of his bishopric in 1688. One of his relatives, Lady Anne Drummond, was married to the Earl of Erroll.

The kirk, erected in 1777, has an interesting link with Ardendraught. Its outer walls were built from a huge granite boulder called the Grey Stone of Ardendraught on which 'Hallow Fires' were once lit. A number of years ago I went to the kirkyard there hoping to find the graves of my grandparents, but it was an impossible task for all that I knew about them was that my grandfather had farmed at Chanonry Knap. What made matters worse was that my father's birth certificate had been lost; it was found again later.

The one thing that stuck in my mind was that my grandmother's maiden name was Margaret Castel, and in the Cruden kirkyard I found the grave of a farmer called Castel. Four of his daughters were buried beside him. The name was Spanish-sounding, raising the intriguing possibility that the Castels were descendants of survivors of the ill-fated *Santa Caterina* or *St Catherine*.

Those who dismiss the *Santa Caterina* story as fanciful say that 'Castel' may simply have been a miss-spelling of the name Castle, but I once saw the old cannon raised from St Catherine's Dub in 1858 (it is kept at Old Slains Castle) and I prefer to cling to the more romantic explanation. The man who raised the cannon was the parish minister of Slains. His name, said Dr Pratt, carefully avoiding making a vulgar quip about it, was Mr Rust. Pratt went on to say that the gun was 'not even corroded'.

My theory about the Castels and Spanish Armada survivors was reinforced by a passage in R. F. Mackenzie's *A Search for Scotland*. In it he described how his sister, while studying medicine at Aberdeen University, met a professor of anatomy who was interested in ethnology. He made physical measurements of his students to find out about their heredity and after measuring her decided that she was of Spanish ancestry. He asked if she had a Spanish grandparent. She said no, but explained what had happened to the *Santa Caterina* near her village. The punchline came at the end of this tale when Mackenzie was pondering on whether or not survivors from the galleon had remained in Scotland, married local girls, and perhaps had given the name of the galleon to a baby daughter. 'Did the name continue until my mother was baptised with the name of Catherine?' he asked.

Castel, Catherine ... I never pursued the matter and the mystery remains. I think I was diverted by another stone in the kirkyard at Cruden. It marked the burial place of James Stewart, a Hatton shoemaker. I remember my father telling me that when he was a young lad at Chanonry Knap he often walked to Hatton to meet up with other farm workers in the souter's back shop. The souter's shop had an important role in village life, as did the tailor's shop, for as well as boots and Sunday suits you could buy necessities of life like sweeties, fags and bogie roll. They were social centres where ferm loons exchanged gossip, talked about the kitchie deems, and gave the farmer's wife her character:

Thin brose and nae breid,
O, God, gin she were deid.

David Toulmin drew a fascinating picture of a souter at work in his *Collected Short Stories*. Here, the souter was Jimmie Duthie, 'the most amazing shoemaker you had ever seen', whose back shop was piled high with boots, its wooden floor 'shovel deep in leather cuttings, shoe nails, iron heels and toe-pieces, discarded protectors, studs, tackets, sprigs, broken bootlaces, and the cigarette packets, match boxes, fag ends and matches thrown down by his various customers'.

Souter Duthie worked mostly at night, hammering away until two or three in the morning:

> He liked working in the evenings when the back shop was full of farm workers and lads from the village, a gathering place for idle youth, when all would flock to Jimmie Duthie's back shop for a news and a blether. Sometimes it was standing room only and the place so thick with fag reek you could hardly see Jimmie at his last by the darkened window, his tilley lamp hanging from a beam in the roof, sizzling away until somebody stood on a chair and pumped more air into it with a brass plunger and its brightened into life again.
>
> But Jimmie never stopped hammering, a string over the boot he was working at to hold it down on the last, looped over the instep of his left foot; his mouth full of sprigs, studs or tackets, taking them in his fingers one by one and plopping them into the new leather he had hammered on to somebody's worn out shoes. Then he would take a seat by the coke stove, waxing thread with rozin and threading his needle, stitching a patch on leatherwork of some bauchled old shoe, for he didn't have a machine and did all his sewing by hand.

When I saw Souter Stewart's tombstone in Cruden kirkyard I wondered if his shop was where my father and his farming pals had gathered for 'a news and a blether', and I went over the Bishop's Brig and on up to Hatton to find out. I got chatting to two old-timers about Buchan souters and one of them remembered a Souter Park in Mintlaw, whose wife had been the local midwife. Park was a bit of a joker. One day a woman came into his shop and asked him if he knew a woman called Park who was a midwife.

'Oh, aye', said Park. 'I slept wi' her last nicht'. The woman turned on her heel and walked out.

A small house in Main Street, with a workshop at one gable-end, was pointed out to me as a former souter's shop. Then I was directed farther up the street to Stan Stewart, who would be able to help me. It turned out that his aunt, Maggie Byres, was a daughter of James Stewart and that the house at No. 9 Main Street had been his home and his workshop.

Maggie, who was born in 1906, lived at 4 Park View, Hatton. She told me that her father had been an Orkney man and that he herded sheep there before moving to Aberdeen to serve his apprenticeship as a shoemaker. Her father, who brought up eight of a family in the Main Street house, was one of four souters in Hatton. Was there work for four souters? 'They a' got a livin',' said Maggie.

William Christie, whose workshop is now a grocer's shop, was another of Hatton's soutering foursome, while a third was George Shewan, who came from Slains. Maggie pointed out a rough corrugated iron shed in a field opposite her house, beside the Water of Cruden. That was where George had finished his days, 'doing shoes'. The fourth souter was Willie Mackie, who had a snooker table in his shop and sold sweets and cigarettes.

There was no drink in James Stewart's shop — he didn't drink himself and didn't allow others to do it on his premises. Generally, drink wasn't a major factor when the farm workers got together. The most social place in Hatton was Walker's the Tailor. Farm servants gathered there and drank lemonade. Maggie remembered them gathering on a Wednesday, which they called 'little Saturday'. That was because on Wednesday the trades people closed their shops to take in stock. It wasn't a full-day closing like Saturday. It was a half-day closing — a little Saturday.

Hatton was the old centre of Cruden parish. It was put on the map by butter biscuits. The man who made them was Forbes Simmer, who moved into the village with £60 and a borrowed horse at the turn of the century and set up a bakery business. The bakery — and the butter biscuits — are still going strong, but not everything has remains unchanged. For one thing, the souters have gone, as have most of the mills driven by Dr Pratt's 'harassed' stream; one is now the Hatton Mill Hotel. The Station Hotel on the Ellon-Peterhead road no longer has a station, its name a reminder of the days when the Ellon-Boddam railway carried wealthy visitors to the luxurious Cruden Bay Hotel.

The name Hatton stands for Hall-town. In the old days, the farmer's house was the Ha', Ha'-hoose, or Ha'toon, which is a pointer to where this peaceful little village had its beginnings on the banks of the Water of Cruden.

CHAPTER FOUR

Down the Buchan Line

When I went down the old Buchan line from Fraserburgh to Maud, following the abandoned railway track south by Lonmay and the Hill of Mormond, I was thinking about two scarecrows. They were the 'twa boodies' in J. C. Milne's poem 'Atomic War', who 'keekit doon fae a star' and saw that Mormond had disappeared. 'Dyod, man', said one to the other, 'faur's yon birlin' earth faur we aince waur?'

That apocalyptic poem, which left you half-way between a laugh and an uneasy shudder, carried a fearful threat which has so far remained unfulfilled, but the end of the world is still not very far from the folk who lived around Mormond. Go down the line to Brucklay Station and you'll find a muddy, rutted farm track off the New Pitsligo road where at one time a wooden sign nailed to a tree read, 'Worldsend − ½ mile'.

The last time I passed that way the birling earth was still there, but the sign had gone. There were new folk in Worldsend, I was told, and I wondered why the name had been removed, for although it was a small farm it had been dignified by a place in the Ordnance Survey maps. I wondered, too, what disillusioned crofter had first thought up such a despairing name for his holding.

Some folk would have you believe that the end of the world is a mile or two farther on in the shanty-town of wooden huts, tin sheds and sprawling sheep pens that marked out Maud as one of the great cattle centres of the North-east. The writer Jack Webster, who was born there, said that some uncharitable people regarded it as the last place on God's earth, but his reply to that was that the good Lord kept the best to the last.

If the 'twa boodies' came back to-day they would find some

30

changes. The trains no longer puff up the Mormond gradient, their smoke getting thicker and blacker with each struggling mile. The lines were lifted when the Beeching axe fell and now the track is beginning to look as it must have done more than a century ago when 300 labourers – Irishmen, Highlanders, Lowland Scots and even Sassenachs from over the Border – hacked and shovelled their way south to build the Buchan railway.

The *Buchan Observer*, commenting on this invasion of burly 'navvies', said delicately, 'Our streets have a very lively appearance'. What the 'Buchany' really meant was that their peace was shattered and that members of the Strichen Total Abstinence Society, stepping over drunken bodies in the gutters, were fighting a losing battle. There was so much crime, immorality and violence that the Strichen police force had to be trebled – from one to three – and eventually two railway policemen were also drafted in. But on Monday, 25 April, 1865, work on the line was completed and it was formally opened.

I set off from Fraserburgh to tramp down this corridor of memories, but despite plans to turn 60 miles of deserted track from Aberdeen to the Broch into a public walkway many sections at the northern end were impassable. The problem, I was told by the Buchan Countryside Group, was that it cost £10,000 to prepare 1 kilometre of track, and on top of that parts of it were still leased to farmers. The Laird of Brucklay, it seemed, was one of the landowners who had no great enthusiasm for walkers marching down his stretch of line.

Brought to an unexpected halt at Brucklay Station, which was once a cattle loading point, I had to get off the track, meanwhile doffing my hat to Dr John Pratt, who had no such trouble when he came that way during his travels. Coming west from Peterhead, he crossed the commutation line from New Deer to Strichen and headed for Banff. He made no mention of Maud, for the simple reason that it didn't exist at that time, but he would have crossed the line of the proposed railway. He died four years after it was opened.

I knew Brucklay well. Alex Murdoch, my uncle, was grieve at Shevado, the home farm, when I was a boy. 'Heaven's in the wid o' Brucklay' went the line of an old song, and for me it was true. I was a toonser, and a tenement toonser at that, and every acre of the Brucklay estate filled me with wonder. I rode with my Uncle Alex in an old truck carrying huge blocks of ice to Brucklay Castle, whose towers and turrets made me curious about the great Laird who lived inside it. I knew that he must have been a powerful man for up on the Hill of Culsh they had raised a huge steeple-like monument to him.

Brucklay has been in the hands of the Dingwall-Fordyce family since 1744, when the estates of Culsh and Brucklay were merged. The castle was built in the 16th century and has had a number of additions in the last centuries. It had 100 rooms and a self-contained cottage on the roof, but its decline began when it became a prisoner-of-war camp during the last war. Heavy rates and repair bills brought about a decision to take its roof off in 1951. Interestingly, the lake was man-made in the 1870s by three men, using only spades and buckets. It took them four years to complete the job.

I remember climbing on to the back of a fat sow at Shevado, scratching its hard hairy skin as it snuffled in the mud and sharn of the piggery. I still have a snapshot showing me sitting astride that 'grumphie', ignoring the warning in the lines of an old bothy song —

A grumphie feedin' in the sty
Wad keep the hoose in greases.

I nibbled at cattle food in a loft above the joiner's shop and wandered down sunlit paths and over tiny fairy-tale bridges spanning the Ugie. At the end of the day I lay in an upstairs bedroom in my uncle's cottage and listened to the melancholy whistle of a Buchan train disappearing into the night.

The railways were Buchan's arteries in those halcyon years between the wars and in Maud, with its great marts, you could hear its heartbeat. Trains came rolling in from Aberdeen, Peterhead and the Broch. 'Change for Fraserburgh', said the sign on the platform, and you climbed into your third-class compartment and went grumbling over the hill to Fraserburgh by way of Satyrhills, a name that made you wonder if some Buchan Dionysus had been chasing the local nymphs up there. There were passengers trains, cattle trains, peat trains, excursion trains, trains for Aikey Fair, and trains crowded with fish girls on their way to Yarmouth and Lowestoft.

My cousin, Sandy Murdoch, son of the Shevado grieve, watched them with wide-eyed wonder. He must have been the youngest railway buff in the country. In 1918, when his parents lived in Strichen, he strayed from the High Street and was found at the Market Leys watching the trains go by. He was only four years old.

Later, during his lunch break at Maud School, he would sneak a look at the trains when running down Station Brae on his way to Mrs Maggie Smith's dining rooms for a plate of mince and tatties. In 1929, when he left school to start his apprenticeship with the local chemist, Charles Anderson, he bought his first camera, a Portrait Brownie, and began to take pictures of the trains.

To-day, into his eighties and still 'snapping' trains, he has published a number of books on North-east 'puffers' and diesels. His *Photographic Memories of the Buchan Line* are a sigh for the days of steam. He recalls how he would watch for a plume of smoke spiralling into the sky on the horizon and, like a hunter watching Indian smoke signals, would give chase until he tracked down his quarry and added another 'scalp' to his collection. There were times when he must have found it difficult, for the sign of a good fireman was 'just a feather of steam from the safety valve and no black smoke'.

For those who might not believe that Maud was once the centre of the Universe, the Central Buchan Tourism Group has put out a leaflet telling — in Doric verse — what the village was like in the good old days. This is one of a number of similar leaflets about Buchan villages and the facts about Maud are impressive. It had two saddlers' shops, three butchers, 'two jiner chiels fa'd mak ye a clyes kist or a cradle', a stone-cutter, two general merchants shops, a chemist 'far ye'd get a dose o' salts', and three tailors. It also had —

Three baker's shops tae keep's supplied
Wi baps an mornin rolls,
Three souters tee tae cater
For the comfort o yer soles.

I remember hearing another local ditty which told how farmers in for the weekly marts would buy such things as wooden posts and binder twine and then go to Lizzie Allan's shoppie 'for sweeties and Wild Woodbine'. It went on —

Kale plants for sale or oil-skin suits,
Or hame they'll gang wi tackety boots.

Down at Station Road I found to my surprise that there was still an old-style souter in the village. 'Henderson's Boot and Shoe Shop' said the sign on the glass door. Stepping into its pine-walled interior was like stepping back ninety years to the day that it opened. Mr Henderson had long since departed. For the last forty-one years Jimmy Christie had been looking after the farmers' soles.

Did he still send them hame wi' tackety boots? 'Na, na', said Jimmy. 'Ye canna get tackets nowadays'.

He was the last of the Maud souters. He believed that when he shut the door for the last time there would be no one else to take his place. I could have done with a pair of tackety boots for the next part of my journey, down the line to Mintlaw, for on the way there I turned off the track, crossed the road and went up Aikey Brae. I was thinking of a pair of lovers who, hand in hand, had gone up that hill some sixty years ago on the day of the great Aikey Fair.

'So you took her by the hand up the brae and set her down among the heather bells, and you thought she was the finest picture in all the fair. There was a kind of sparkle in her soft eyes that was maybe worth more than diamonds, and a velvet gloss on her hair as it tumbled about in the sun glint, with maybe a bit coloured ribbon in it, trying to beguile a daft gowk like yourself that had been looking all the week at a mare's tail tied up with segs.

'She had a straw hat with a red band and a checked tweed coat, but as it was a stifling day these lay beside her on the heather; and there she sat with bare arms in a print frock, net stockings and brown brogue shoes, her smiling lips reminding you of comb-dripped honey and a scent about her like carnations, shy and blushing as a sunrise. Ah well, when you'd had your fill of looking at the quine and listening to the music of her laugh, and maybe stealing a kiss on the sly, you'd take her hand again and you'd dander down to the fair'.

The tale of that lad and lass courting at Aikey Fair was told in *Collected Short Stories*, by David Toulmin, the farm loon who became one of the great chroniclers of North-east life. Two or three days before walking the Buchan line I had been having a dram with Toulmin (or John Reid, as I knew him) and we were talking about his anthology. I mentioned one of his stories, 'The Dookit Fairm', and jokingly asked John's wife, Margaret, if she had been the model for Elsie Wabster, who wore the breeks and 'was aye oot yappin at the back kitchie door'. No, no, she said, she had often been taken for some of the characters in the Toulmin stories, but, in fact, she had featured in only one. That was 'Aikey Brae'.

So she was the 'blushing quine' who accompanied John 'up the brae, out of the steer, up among the heather and the smell of fresh peat'. Now, sixty years later, she was preparing for their diamond wedding. I lifted my glass to toast the happy couple.

I went on to Mintlaw, thinking about Aikey and how it had once been, the noise of it dirling your ears, the hurdy-gurdy organ grinding out 'That Ole Black Mammy o Mine', and the riders on the Wall of Death flying round and round 'like a bool in a brose caup'. When I got to Mintlaw I passed

the shop where an uncle of mine had worked as a souter —
'W. Cockburn, Boot and Shoemaker' — charging the princely
sum of 6d for 'boots patched'. In more recent years my camera-
carrying cousin ran the local pharmacy in Mintlaw. His house
and shop overlooked the huge Mintlaw roundabout, a monstrous merry-go-round that the newspapers called the
Piccadilly of Buchan when it was first built. It made you feel
as if you were embarking on a circular tour of the village
before being pitched out at whatever road you were taking. I
was taking the road to Longside and Peterhead.

The railway clings to the road between Mintlaw and
Longside, passing Crookedneuk, where the old Glenugie distillery was 'fast falling into decay' when Dr Pratt saw it. At
Auchlee Bridge I crossed the South Ugie Water and went
down to Longside. Like Mintlaw, this 'new town' was founded at the turn of the century, but it has always seemed to me
to retain a good deal more of the old village character than
its neighbour. Perhaps it is Mintlaw's Piccadilly roundabout,
out of place and out of time, that disturbs me. David Toulmin
had a soft spot for Longside parish, 'where the pastures are
fresh and the waters are musical'. He was drawn to it, he said,
because it 'nurtured an esoteric few who left their names on
the escutcheon of fame', men like John Skinner of 'Tulloch-
gorum', John Imray, and Peter Still, the Bard of Ugieside.

When I walked through Longside I half-expected to hear
the voice of another of Toulmin's 'esoteric few' calling to me,
asking 'Fa's feel are e'e?' Jamie Fleeman, the Laird o' Udny's
fool, is buried in the local kirkyard a stone's throw from the
main street. Inscribed on an obelisk is his dying request,
'Dinna bury me like a beast'. They didn't, and Jamie lies in
good company, for John Skinner was buried in the same kirkyard. His cottage at Linshart, where he preached from a window after his church was burned, is half a mile south of the
village.

Back on the railway line I was looking for the site of a
cottage called Poynerneuk on the farm of Mains of Buthlaw.
It had been built of stone and clay and had a straw thatched

roof, while near it was a 'wee housie' called the 'John Gunn' —
the old name for an outside toilet. Ninety years ago, five-year-
old Janet Thomson and her brother, William, who was four,
left Poynerneuk and set out to tramp the two miles to
Longside for their first day at school.

Kitty Reid, from Tarves, who guided me in my wanderings
in the Longside area, had a special interest in Poynerneuk, for
Janet Thomson was her mother. Janet and her family were
using the old Buchan line as a walkway long before anyone
ever thought of doing it for pleasure. It was not uncommon for
her father, Robert Thomson, to walk six miles along the track
to get the local 'vet' when a cow was having a difficult birth.

What must have been one of the longest walks on the old
Buchan railway took place before the First World War. Kitty
Reid's father, William Reid, who worked on his father's croft
near Longside, was h'yowin'neeps with another farm worker
near the line when he decided that this was not for him. He
threw down his hoe and declared that he was packing it in —
he was going to join the Army.

'I'll gae wi' ye', said his companion. 'Fan are ye jinin'!'?'

'Now!' said Bill.

Together they crossed the field to the railway track and
looked to the left, where it went off to Peterhead, then to the
right, where it spun away to Aberdeen. They stepped on to
the line, turned right, and walked more than thirty miles to
the city to enlist in the Gordon Highlanders.

Bill lied about his age to get into the Gordons — he was
only seventeen. A few years later war broke out. The farm
loon who had become a 'sodjer' fought through it and came
out at the end of it with the Croix de Guerre (Belgian) and
Military Medal. He never went back to hyowin'.

Kitty's Uncle Willie, the wee boy who had gone off to
school with his sister Janet, started *his* working life as an
ostler at the Bruce Arms in Longside. From there he went to
a place I knew well — Brucklay Castle — to be trained as a butler. The war put an end to that and when it was over his career
lay in other directions. In the Spring of 1979, while living at

Kemnay, he wrote an account of his schooldays in Buchan between 1902 and 1911.

Willie Thomson wrote 'Schooldays in Buchan' for his family, but it is a fascinating social document, providing a valuable record of life in the Howe of Buchan in the early years of this century. It brings to life many of the old Buchan characters, like 'Fusslin' Davie', who carried a small box of trinkets and always whistled through his teeth. Davie was another man who did a marathon walk through Buchan. He had been in prison in Aberdeen and on his release one morning he set off for Longside on foot. He took a short cut *through* the River Ythan to avoid a long loop by Ellon.

Newseat was a wayside railway halt about a mile east of Poynerneuk. During the last war it was used by RAF personnel from the nearby fighter station, and in post-war years the airfield became a heliport operating for the oil industry. Back in the days when the Thomsons were at Poynerneuk it was a stopping-off point for fish-wives from Buchanhaven, then an independent fisher-town north of Peterhead. Peter Buchan, whose mother came from Buchanhaven, once told me that there was so much fish in the sea there that the boats came in every day laden with haddock.

Some of these haddocks went up the Buchan line to Longside. Willie Thomson recalled how the fish-wives came from Peterhead by train, got off at one station and worked their way to the next, and went back on the early afternoon train with a good supply of bartered eggs. He remembered a fish-wife who called regularly at Poynerneuk with a creel on her back and one, sometimes two baskets over her arms. In the herring season there were men with ponies and floats shouting, 'Herrin', caller herrin'!' and chasing each other to catch the trade.

In 1910, Willie's father left the Mains of Buthlaw to become grieve on the estate of Cairngall. The family moved to Woodend, 'a bigger house with an upstairs bedroom and an attic or garret'. This was his description of the 410-acre farm:

There was a herd of around 40 pedigree Shorthorn breeding cows and their followers; about 100 other cattle; four pairs of working horses and 2–3 spare ones, also the young home-bred ones. There were eight regular men and an additional two for harvest. There was a bothy where the single men got their food. This was looked after by the bothy 'deem' and her younger assistant. Apart from cooking they milked the 5–6 cows three times daily and dished out the milk to the cottars and laird's house.

The laird's mother and sister lived in a nearby house and were supplied with all farm produce, milk, butter, eggs, poultry and the occasional half sheep. The bothy women had therefore to make butter, dress poultry and supply milk to both houses, which between them had also five maids to be catered for. I've omitted to mention that there was a flock of up to a hundred breeding ewes.

Cairngall House is on the outskirts of Longside, a long low 18th-century granite house refashioned in the early 19th century. The present farmer of Cairngall is Neil Godsman, whose son works the farm of Auchlee, on the north side of the Buchan line.

As I was heading for the Blue Toon I was thinking of the folk in Willie Thomson's manuscript, humbler folk engaged in less weighty ploys, like my namesake, Bob Smith, who was a cattleman at Cairngall and had musical inclinations. He and his wife cycled round the district on a tandem bike bringing music to the ferm touns. The music came from a phonograph, the kind of 'instrument' my old music teacher used to wind up and introduce as 'music by Handel'. Bob Smith carried it on his back, along with the records.

There was another travelling minstrel in Willie's story, 'Dancie' Sim, who was a mason and lived at New Pitsligo. Dancing masters were all the rage in those days. 'Dancie' Sim cycled about the countryside with his fiddle on his back, thinking nothing of a 20-mile round trip on a winter's night to take a class. Willie and Janet Thomson were among his pupils. He played his fiddle while demonstrating the steps and taught the boys how to bow properly when they asked the girls if they would care to dance.

The North Ugie Water comes sweeping down from the Pitsligo bogs and wriggles its way to the sea between the Mains of Buthlaw and Middleton of Rora. This stretch of the river near the junction of the North and South Ugie was a happy hunting ground for pearl fishers. In his memoir, Willie wrote about the nomadic Stewarts, who went around rag collecting and lived in 'an igloo tent'. Donald, the father, who had a flowing white beard, was a piper and had three sons, also pipers. One had been blinded in South Africa.

'In summer they spent a lot of time pearl fishing', said Willie. 'The blind one rowed the tub of a boat, while the other two leant over the sides holding their special glasses in the water searching for the big oysters to be found in the Ugie. I never heard of them finding a pearl, but by the law of averages they must have done, judging by the heaps of shells left on the riverbanks'.

Willie Thomson died in 1981. The document he left behind threw light on a way of life that has long since disappeared. Poynerneuk is no more, and other places that he wrote about have changed beyond recognition. He looked back to a time when they lived 'in the midst of what would be termed near-poverty', yet the things that he remembered most were happiness and contentment.

CHAPTER FIVE

Pitfour and Aden

They called it the Garden of Buchan. It was one of the North-east's great estates, spreading out from the South Ugie Water and covering 33,000 acres of rich Buchan farmland. Its 18th century mansion house was an architectural oddity, fashioned more from the calendar than from a planner's blueprint. It had 365 windows, one for each day of the year, fifty-two rooms for the weeks of the year, and four staircases for the changing seasons. When a portico was added it had twelve pillars — one for each month of the year.

Pitfour was the home of the Ferguson family. They lived in style, created an enormous lake, scattered rocco statues about the estate, built magnificent stables and lodges, laid out a race-course and an observatory, dug a canal from Pitfour to the sea (parts of it can still be seen near Inverugie), and won a repu-tation for lavish spending and irresistible eccentricity. The estate was purchased in 1700 by James Ferguson, an advocate at the Scottish bar. He was the first of six Ferguson lairds in the two centuries that followed.

Today the estate has shrunk to 457 acres, yet it still retains something of the magic that made Buchan's historian, Dr John Pratt, marvel at its 'shrubberies, ornamental flower-gardens, carriage-drives, winding footpaths and *jets d'eau*'. He declared it 'one of the most distinguished residences in the district' and it is a judgement that still stands. The House with 365 windows has long since gone, demolished in 1927, and now the focal point of the estate is a former Episcopal rectory, which Admiral George Ferguson, the fifth Laird, turned into a Dower House for his mother-in-law, Frances Baroness Langford.

It stands above the Ugie on Saplin Brae, whose name was once chanted in an old rhyme —

At Sapling Brae
I brak' my tae
I shod my horse at Biffie . . .

The Dower House is now an elegant country house hotel, run by Bill and Dorothy Adam, who previously had an engineering company in Peterhead. Bill is in the oil business. Until they took over the house and turned it into a hotel in 1982 little had been done to it by previous owners. 'What you see now is what we've done in the past ten years', said Dorothy. Extensive restoration work has been carried out on both the house and the estate, which she believes was laid out in the style of Capability Brown. Pitfour's charm has cast a spell over the Adams. 'We are besotted with this place', she said.

Climbing into her powerful four-wheel drive to take a look at Dr Pratt's 'carriage drives, winding footpaths and *jets d'eau*' (jet of water), I thought of the rhymster who had shod his horse at Biffie. He had passed this way —

I poo'd a wand
On Benwal's yard
An whuppit on to Bruxie.

The names in the rhyme were the names of farms, but Bruxie Lodge is one of two lodges guarding the estate. The South Lodge, the main entrance, faces a wall erected as a monument to the Younger Pitt and to Henry Dundas, Lord Melville. The man who erected it was James Ferguson, the third laird, who became MP for Aberdeenshire in 1790 and eventually Father of the House of Commons. He was also responsible for laying out Pitfour Lake, a hugely beautiful stretch of water near the South Lodge. We rode across two stone bridges built to carry the main drive over the lake to the old Mansion House.

James Ferguson was a small, fat, good-humoured man who

wore a long high-collared surcoat and old-fashioned knee breeches. His ideas were far from old-fashioned. He probably did more for Pitfour, and for Buchan, than all the other lairds put together. He played a major role in introducing turnpike roads to Buchan, and he 'planted many hundreds of acres, enclosed whole farms with hawthorn hedges, and granted leases to all his tenants on terms peculiarly liberal'.

Ferguson's inspiration for Pitfour Lake was the building by the Prince Regent of an artificial lake in Windsor Park. The Prince later added a Temple made from antique columns and from this sprang the laird's decision to build Pitfour's first 'folly', a miniature copy of the famous Temple of Theusu at Athens. It is in a slightly sad state now, supported by scaffolding, for the cost of repair runs to £62,000, but Dorothy Adam plans to do it at some time in the future.

Behind the Temple a path goes down through a secluded woodland area known as the Low Gardens, laid out with rare trees, including cypress, and this, too, will be restored. It was there that Mrs Adam found a mineral well, which will form part of the Temple Garden. I discovered later that there were *two* chalybeate springs in the Low Gardens, which were used for medicinal purposes in the old days, so Pitfour may one day become the Pannanich of Buchan.

As we 'whuppit on to Bruxie', driving around the lake and looking across its placid waters to three small islands, we could see a pair of swans and their eight cygnets below us, a reminder that not long after the lake was built a colony of swans and wild duck landed on it and began to use it as a breeding ground. The lake was stocked with Loch Leven trout and today trout fishing by boat on the 37 acre lake is one of the facilities offered to visitors.

We passed part of the estate where the Adams had planted 22,000 trees and we came to a piece of open ground where grass and flowers grew wild, knee-high. It had been left that way because it had become a haven for birds. This, it turned out, was where the old Mansion House had been, but there was nothing to show that it had ever existed. Until recently the open basement could be seen, but it was dangerous and had been filled in. From this spot, looking out from one of its 365 windows, the Laird and his family had a view clear across the lake. A ferry service operated between the house and the Temple.

The only link with those far-off days was a huge tree which, stripped of its foliage, reached skeleton arms towards the site of the house. Old photographs of the mansion show the tree spreading out majestically on the east side of the portico. When Mrs Adam's four-year-old grand-daughter, Brittany, saw this gaunt old trunk she said it was a Disney-world tree.

A Disney-world tree . . . and a Disney-world house. Standing there, I was thinking of the idiosyncratic Admiral who became the fifth Laird of Pitfour. George Ferguson loved his Buchan home. He and his family came to the Mansion House in July and usually stayed till February or March. He fished in the lake and shot in the fields and woods. He was proud of Pitfour, but he was largely responsible for its downfall.

He carried out great alterations and additions at Pitfour, built stables which were said to 'straddle the skyline like a palace' (they are now on Alan Watson's neighbouring farm at Chapel Park), and opened a riding school. After that came the Ascot of Buchan — a racecourse, $4^{1}/_{2}$ miles long, which swept in a great circle from Cairnorchies through White Cow, Auchrynie, Cabra and Gaval. Then came the Observatory, a high tower (now in the care of the district council and open to the public) from which the Laird watched the races and placed bets with his coterie of London friends. He was an addictive gambler, making frequent trips to Paris and Naples to try his luck in the gambling houses there, while back at Pitfour his gambling parties were the talk of the neighbourhood.

Bailiffs, forty foresters, coachmen, stablemen, grooms, kennelmen, butlers, footmen, gardeners, gamekeepers, cooks and maids . . . he had an army of servants to look after his needs. It was said that a sheep was killed every day and a bullock every week for the household. The Pitfour fortunes slipped away. Income never covered expenditure, land was sold, loans raised, his wife's jointure was cut from £3000 a year to £1500. His death in 1867 passed almost unnoticed. The *Times* carried nothing; his local paper, the *Buchan Observer*, carried only ten lines.

When I left Pitfour I went down to the Ugie, where a curious bridge crosses the river near the Abbey of Deer. One half of it is wider than the other. This came about as the result of an argument between the Fergusons and the Russells of Aden over the building of the Pitfour lake. The Russells claimed that it would bring flooding to Aden, but their fears were ignored. They got their revenge when the Fergusons widened their half of the bridge so that coaches could cross it. The Russells refused to widen *their* half — and the result can still be seen today.

From the bridge I made my way to Aden, which was once owned by James Ferguson of Kinmundy, a cousin of the Pitfour Ferguson, who sold it to Alexander Russell of Montcoffer in 1758. He was a progressive laird, paving the way for succeeding generations of Russells, who enlarged what was a modest mansion, added a coach-house and gate lodges, and built a unique semi-circular steading with a three-storey central tower. The lands of Kininmonth and Ludquharn were added to the estate, which covered 31 square miles.

Aden, like Pitfour, went into decline, but more slowly, and in 1937 the last laird, Sidney Russell, sold the estate, much of Old Deer, and fifty-two farms. In the years that followed the grounds were neglected and the buildings became derelict, but in 1975 Banff and Buchan District Council set about reversing the process. The steading was renovated and turned into a heritage centre and the policies became Aden Country Park, which each year draws thousands of visitors to this corner of Buchan.

The years slipped away and the images faded. Now you look at the great shell of Aden House and wonder what life was like when the Russells lived there, cosseted by an army of servants who were kept on their toes by 'Missie', Sidney

Russell's mother, who wore 'lang black cla'es' and was a bit of a 'thristle' — testy and crabbed. Not long after the Country Park was opened I met two old-timers who were at Aden in the 1920s. Charlie Hendry was a kennelman and George Birnie was a foreman gardener. Both were seventy-one.

They drifted off into their yesterdays, Charlie recalling 'the old duchess', which was his name for 'Missie'. She didn't like 'steer', she counted the apples on the garden trees to see if any had been stolen, and when she was there at Christmas none of the servants' bairns got presents. They remembered the Laird as a man to keep clear of when he had a gun in his hand. 'When you handed him a double-barrelled gun', said Charlie, 'you kept weel awa'. He wasted more ammunition than you've ever seen in your life'. Sadly, Charlie died a few years ago.

George remembered Sidney's nephew, 'wee Willie White-law', coming to Aden in the 1920s. He was about twelve at the time — 'jist a loon'. Fifty years later, Willie Whitelaw had become Viscount Whitelaw and returned to Aden to officially open the Country Park. Now, wee Willie's cousin, James Russell, the only surviving son of Sidney Russell, makes regular visits to Aden — and crosses the Ugie to stay in the old Ferguson home at the Saplinbrae House Hotel.

On that first visit to Aden I met Mary Jane Thomson, whose father had worked for the Russells for £72 a year, plus three pints of milk a day. Mary Jane was acting as a costume guide, a kind of latter-day 'horseman's wife', in the Horseman's House, where she had lived as a small child. When I went back in 1995 she had stepped down and her place had been taken by another Thomson, Helen Thomson, who, like her predecessor, was baking oatcakes on the open fire.

Nobody makes oatcakes that way nowadays, so I ate a piece hot off the girdle. Helen said she sometimes made oatcakes at home, but they never tasted like the ones she baked on the girdle in the Horseman's House, and I could understand why. She had an unmistakable Buchan tongue and we got to talking about the old Doric words, the ones you never hear nowadays – and are not likely to hear again. Helen never slips into Doric when parties of schoolchildren visit the Horseman's House; she talks 'proper'. If you launched into Doric, she said, they wouldn't understand a word you said.

Later, I was catapulted back through the years by Albert Brown, who, as well as looking after 200 head of cattle on his farm at Mitchell Hill, Maud, acts as a guide at the Hareshowe Working Farm at Aden. Here, starting at the neep shed, uneducated toonsers can learn about the Buchan farmer's year, about crop rotation on the farm's six 3-acre fields, and about all the farming paraphernalia that has been swept away by new equipment and new farming methods ... everything from an old threshing machine to a souter's last, from peat spades and harrows to an dilapidated railway carriage used as a store. When space was short one end of it was turned into a bedroom.

But Hareshow is relatively modern. I wanted to know more about life in the Big House. Andrew Hill, Principal Curator, Aberdeenshire Heritage, opened the door for me. He had in his files an inventory and valuation of *everything* in Aden in the year 1875. In this remarkably detailed document column after column marked off all the property of 'the deceased James Russell Esquire of Aden Aberdeenshire who died at Aberdeen on the Eighteenth day of January Eighteen Hundred and Seventy five years'. It provided a fascinating insight into how the Lairds of Aden lived more than a century ago, the food they ate, the jewellery their womenfolk wore, the cutlery on the table, the books in the library, the kettles and pans in the kitchen, the dogcarts and phaetons in the coach house, the children's cribs in the nursery. The wine cellar made you hiccup; champagne, port, claret, sherry . . . gallons of the stuff, rounded off with a 'Cask and about 2 Gals. Whisky', costing £1 10.

Like some 19th-century peeping Tom I wandered through the pages of the inventory learning about the Russells and their servants, about the footman and the butler, the cooks and the housemaids. I found myself in the blue bedroom, which had a mahogany four-poster bed, and into the red bed-room, whose occupants had bed steps and a sitting bath, and I opened the housemaid's pantry and found a copper bed warmer, a bidet (damaged) and a chamber pedestal. Then I slipped into Mrs Russell's boudoir, which boasted a corner whatnot and a small whatnot. Whatnots were portable stands with shelves, used for displaying ornaments, and Mrs Russell had plenty of ornaments to display — sixty-six on the mantel-piece alone!

She must have been a bookish lady, for the inventory shows that she had 287 volumes of books in her room, along with book stands, book shelves and a book frame. There were also twenty-seven prints and photographs — and a con-certina. I wondered if it had been the Laird's wife herself who played the 'squeezebox'. Did she sit in her boudoir and pump out some melancholy ballad while her husband puffed at a big cigar in the smoking room and talked about his day on the moors?

A separate inventory for farm, stable and farm stock, dated 1887, took me away from boudoirs and bedrooms to barns and bothies, and it was here that the gamekeepers' department had its tally . . . guns, dogs (two pointers and a retriever), dog houses, hutches, hampers and a ferret box. The labourers' department had more down-to-earth items like turfing irons, cleeks, hoes, rakes, handbills and scythes, while another sec-tion took care of the carriages . . . a landau, a brougham, a victoria, a dog cart, a whitechapel cart, a phaeton — and an omnibus costing £40.

So it went on — an inventory of Buchan history, a picture of life in one of its great houses painted from a palette of cold facts and figures. The way of life reflected in the pages of the inventory began to slip away in the years between the wars. Aden, with its small army of servants, started its downward slide after the first world war when three-quarters of the estate was sold off. With farm income falling and maintenance costs rising, the last resident laird, Sidney Russell, saw the writing on the wall. In 1937 he sold the estate.

Life at Aden in this final period is mirrored in a series of photographs which were acquired in a way that is still shrouded in mystery. In 1988, Andrew Hill got a phone call from a Sergeant Toby Stobbart, who worked for the Hampshire police. He thought they would be interested in the recovery of a photograph album in their lost property department. It had been there for some time and was due to be destroyed, but Sgt. Stobbart had discovered a link with a place called Aden at Mintlaw in Scotland.

Andrew sent on a £5 note to cover postage and the album duly arrived. There was no name on it and no indication of who owned it, but the photographs in the album were of the Russells of Aden, not only family photographs, but photographs of Sidney Russell's wedding, including a shot of a page-boy, aged five. His name — William Whitelaw. In September, 1994, when James Russell came north to see Aden he was asked about the album. It was, he said, one of two albums that had belonged to his mother, who died in 1978. To this day no one knows what had happened to it in its ten lost years — or how it came to be found in a village green in Hampshire, England.

The photographs in the album go back to 1922, when Sidney Russell was married in London to Meriel Fetherstonhaugh, of Westmeath, Ireland. The bride, said one newspaper report, was attended by two small boys, one of them being Master William Whitelaw, who is seen clutching the hand of a flower girl carrying a posie of primroses. Wee Willie was dressed in long blue trousers and a cream crêpe de Chine shirt. Meanwhile, back in Buchan, a bonfire was lit on Aikey Brae and a cheering crowd toasted the health of the newly-weds. It was the beginning of the last chapter in the story of the Russells of Aden.

CHAPTER SIX

Strichen House

The old mansion house stood in the middle of rain-soaked farmland, hemmed in by a sea of mud. The house had become a shell, its roof gone, its shattered gable-end gaping like a raw wound. Inside, dust and rubble. Outside, the final indignity ... a crude concrete and corrugated-iron barn erected along the length of the building. I wondered if Mormond Tam was turning in his grave ...

It was early February when I went to Strichen House. 'You'll need "wellies",' said the farmer at the Mains, but I needed more than that. Glaur lay like thick porridge in front of the house and snow and heavy rain had created a miniature lake. Picking my way over the mud I felt my foot sink and then, with a great squelch, I was up to my knees in muck and water.

Carol Bambrough, who lives at the Gardener's Cottage, had told me it was dangerous. I should have heeded her, and I paid the price, but I hauled myself out, emptied my boots, and went on. Inside the barn, bales of hay were stored almost to the ceiling, covered by sheets of black plastic. Small strips of the material had been ripped off by the wind and blown on to a nearby tree, where they hung from the branches like ghoulish black crows. They reminded me of the dead birds that farmers hang on their fences.

Strichen House was designed in 1821 for Thomas Fraser of Strichen, later Lord Lovat, who was known as Mormond Tam. After the new towns and the agricultural improvements of the mid and late 18th century, a fresh wave of prosperity swept through the North-east at the turn of the century. The result was a rash of neo classical mansions in Buchan and

Banff, great houses like Strichen, Pitfour, Aden, Crimonmogate, Glasshaugh and Mountblairy; some austere, some elegant, some noble, but all made to last. Not many did.

From a high grassy bank near the old Buchan railway line I looked down on the sodden field in front of the house. Rhododendron bushes were growing there, great clusters of them stretching away to a knoll called Uncle's Hillock, where a deserted chapel still stands. Dead or dying trees seemed to lift their branches despairingly to the gloomy sky and it was difficult to believe that all this was once beautiful parkland laid out by the English landscape gardener Gilpin. But on that grey February day the first buds were appearing. Soon, the rhododendron bushes would bloom again, a great splash of colour would flood over the scene, and for a short time the past would come alive.

I stood on broken masonry at the gable-end of the mansion, looking into the house, and shuddered at what had happened to Mormond Tam's dream. The house had three storeys, with only two showing above the ground. The floor at ground level had been torn out, or had simply rotted away, and through a great hole in it the lower floor or basement could be seen, with doors to store rooms, or, perhaps, to the wine cellar.

There had been forty-five rooms in the house. I could see part of a stairway leading down to the hall, all that was left of a magnificent double staircase, 15ft. wide, where the guests in all their finery descended from their bedrooms, nodding to the Dukes of Argyll, whose portraits in full Highland regalia lined the stairway, along with that of the Frasers of Strichen in their red kilts. Many of the pictures were the work of George Jameson, the Aberdeen portrait painter, who was hailed as the Scottish van Dyke.

Standing there, watching the wind stir the dust in the ruins of that once-magnificent mansion, I wondered what Lady Cauldock would have thought of it all. She would have come sweeping down those stairs, pulling her shawl more closely around her shoulders, muttering about the climate in that awful place. Lady Cauldock! Only someone from Buchan could have thought up that nickname for the wife of the Laird of Strichen — 'an English wife', said Christian Watt. She got it because it was said that even in the hottest summer she always kept her nether regions warm with two pairs of flannel drawers. The fiery Christian, who was never known to mince her words, once told her that her heart was 'as cold as your backside is reputed to be'. She preferred to stay on the Lovat estate at Beauly, where the climate was milder, coming to Strichen for the shooting with 'bigwigs like the Duke of Norfolk and well-moneyed Catholics from France'.

Christian once angrily reminded the Laird that his fine art collection came 'from the sweat of thousands of human beings, both in Buchan and Jamaica', and that his £70,000 mansion house was built 'from the fruits of a slave plantation belonging to your grandfather, Menzies of Culdares'. She told him that at the wages he paid his servants — $3^1/_2$d for a 17-hour day — it would take ordinary people between sixteen and seventeen thousand years to cover the price of such a house. 'You are making pretty sure we never get up alongside you', she declared.

By all accounts, Mormond Tam was a kindly enough man, but he liked money, had considerable ambition, and was ingrained with the aristocrat's traditional notions of rank and privilege. He was sure that God had set him above ordinary mortals. When he was angry or upset he had a tendency to stutter — 'habber', said Christian Watt — and Christian gave him much to habber about. She could never understand how the wealthy classes had the hard neck to enter any church and call themselves Christians. 'God will spew them out of his mouth', she declared.

She thought that Strichen House was one of the most beautiful mansions in Scotland, the estate one of the finest, but she had no illusions about where the cottars fitted into this Buchan idyll. They had been heritors of rented land, broken in from the heather in the promising days of the 'new towns'; now Mormond Tam had bought out their holdings and they had become 'scab wage earners in a tied house'. It was a situation that was to worsen when the estate changed hands.

From the ruins of Strichen House I could see across the fields to Mormond. Christian Watt had seen new parks 'marching up the side of Mormond Hill', but with the passing of the years the greed for land had grown so much that the crofters found their holdings being snatched away from them. The lairds and the big farmers were 'consolidating', taking over reclaimed land and showing little sympathy for what happened to the crofters. The rents were high and the end of a lease always brought an increase in them.

When the Lovats moved north to Beauly in 1855 they sold the estate to George Baird, of the Gartsherrie Iron Works. The crofters had cause to rue the change in ownership. 'Whole farms were made out of crofts from which the previous occupiers had to move', wrote William Alexander in 1868 in his *Rural Life in Victorian Aberdeenshire*, 'many of these having reclaimed their land from the side of Mormond Hill; and now there are only about twenty crofts remaining in the whole parish. No compensation was given for reclaiming the land, half a year's rent, merely, being allowed for the value of the houses built'.

Over 100 small holdings in the former Lovat estate were wiped out. John Sleigh, the Strichen factor, explained this away by saying that the increased price of labour and manure had made it impossible for the small crofters to live. 'They have been simply breeding up a race of paupers', he said, 'and consequently a great many of the crofts have been consolidated; a great many new steadings and farm-houses have been built, and some of the old crofters' houses have been left standing for the accommodation of the farm servants'.

There is an apocryphal story that the local minister, disturbed by the ruthlessness shown by the new owner of the Strichen estate, asked him, 'Where are the poor people to go?'

'They may go to hell for me', was the reply.

'If you really want to put them permanently out of your

way', said the minister, 'I think you had better send them in the opposite direction'.

Back in 1763, Mormond Tam's great-grandfather, Lord Strichen, advertised his intention to establish a 'new town' in the lap of Mormond Hill, a place with 'an inexhaustible supply of moss, a weekly market, and four Great Fairs annually'. It would be 'within six Miles of nine Fish-towns' and would be 'a most convenient Receptacle for all Persons'. More than a century later, they were talking about clearing out crofters who had 'made' their land with more or less success and were now 'living in miserable hovels, not a few of them little better than semi-barbarians', apt to merge into pauperism and become a burden on the rates.

From the Gardener's Cottage a path leads up through a field and past a ruined Doocot to the Strichen Stone Circle. Boswell and Johnson went out of their way to see it while travelling to the Hebrides in 1773. The celebrated duo dined at Strichen House, but Boswell wasn't filled with envy over the Frasers life-style in their Grecian mansion. When they left Strichen he told Dr Johnson that he had 'a most disagreeable notion of the life of country gentlemen', adding, 'I left Mr Fraser just now as one leaves a prisoner in jail'. Dr Johnson said he was right in thinking them unhappy; they didn't have enough to 'keep their minds in motion'.

Nor were they over-impressed with the famous stone circle. Only two stones remained, up-ended and with a long one on top of them. The main stone in the circle was a short distance away. Carol Bambrough told me that at one time the stones were removed by farmers, but Lord Lovat ordered them to be put back. They *were* put back — on the wrong site. Finally, they were returned to their rightful place when a team of volunteers re-erected them in 1981.

In the summer a good many visitors tramp past Carol's door on their way to the Stone Circle. Mostly, they are from abroad, and they come to see the Circle and not Strichen House. It lies behind them, brooding at the bottom of the brae. From the top of the brae there is a fine view of

Aden House, pictured from the main drive, October 1929
(*Aberdeenshire Museums*).

The Home Farm, Aden, May 1927 (*Aberdeenshire Museums*).

Aden Heritage Centre.

Thatched cottage near Stuartfield.

Stuartfield and the village bell.

Village pump at Stuartfield.

Shooter and keepers with part of
the bag after a shoot over
Ludquharn Moor on the Aden
estate, 20 August 1924
(*Aberdeenshire Museums*).

The author as a lad, on the
back of a Clydesdale at
Cauldwells Farm.

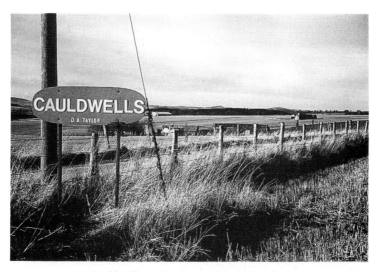

Cauldwells — the sign at the road-end.

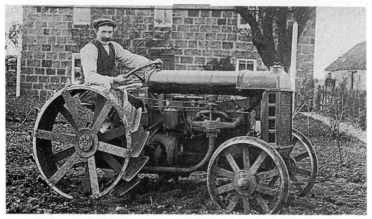

A Fordson Model F tractor bought in 1919 by George Bruce,
Overside, St Fergus (*George Bruce*).

The hairst at Rora in the 1930s (*W. J. Bruce*).

The author as a lad (left) . . . on the back of a 'grumphie' at the
farm of Shevado, Maud.

Ruined Brucklay Castle.

Pitfour Arms Hotel.

Strichen Hotel.

Sheila Smith the author's wife, at the Sands of Forvie.

All that is left of the croft of Cairnywink (Karny Wynke).

Ruined tailor's shop at Muirtack.

The Karne.

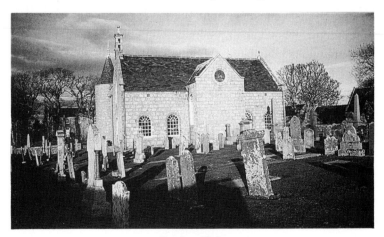

Charlie Adamson and granddaughter.

Cruden Kirk.

Kinnaird Head Lighthouse.

Inverallochy Castle.

Broadsea.

Phillip and Pam Miller outside Cairness House.

Crimonmogate House.

Hillhead of Seggat.

Mrs Joyce Singer at Meiklebogs.

Jim Hunter outside the Brounhill Bothy.

Andy Taylor beside blocked-in bothy door at Cauldwells.

David Taylor and son Mark at Cauldwells.

New Byth.

Jim Allan at Granite Croft. Francie's house was in the trees.

Peggy Clark at the Shalloch.

Delgatie Castle.

Captain Hay with unicorn.

Alec and Dorothy Clark outside Montcoffer House.

Bridge of Alvah.

Eden Castle.

Duff House.

Francie Jamieson.

Mormond Hill and its White Horse. The Rev. Andrew Chalmers, a Buchan minister who was well-known for his attacks on the 'needlessly ostentatious' lairds, called Mormond his Holy Hill. He saw it 'like the face of a familiar friend', which perhaps explains why Buchan folk have an unassailable affection for this modest peak. I have always thought that Strichen should have been allowed to keep its original name, Mormond, instead of having the Laird's name thrust on it.

The end of the Fraser era was not the end of Strichen House. First came the Bairds of Gartsherrie, who held it until the end of last century. The famous Edwardian actress Lillie Langtry was a friend of Abingdon Baird, which must have set male hearts fluttering in Strichen toon. After that it was let out as a shooting lodge, and one of its best-known tenants was the Aberdeen opera star Mary Garden. In 1926 an English syndicate bought the house and its 160-acre estate and opened the Strichen House Hotel, better known to locals as 'The Hydro'.

You could have a special suite at the Hydro at a weekly rate of £8 8s (£8.40 in today's money) and if you wanted a private sitting room it cost you 10s (50p). There was an artificial lake in which you could fish for trout, two tennis courts, and a nine-hole golf course. The hotel closed in 1929 and the nine-hole golf course was ploughed up. During the last war Strichen House was used to billet British, Norwegian and Polish troops, and in 1954 it was gutted.

The town of Strichen lies in the valley of the North Ugie and is said to be the finest example of a large planned village in Buchan. When Lord Strichan established it one of his declared aims was to 'promote the arts' as well as the 'manufactures of this country'. This lordly ambition was realised in a way he could never have foreseen, for two centuries later Strichen has become the cultural heart of Buchan, home of the Buchan Heritage Festival and the Doric Drama Festival. Here, in May, the music of fiddles, melodeons, pianos and pipes sounds throughout the village, while, in poem and play, voices keep alive the rich Doric of Buchan.

So I left Strichen toon, sad at how its great mansion house had slumped into decay, but glad that this was a 'new town' that had done well for itself, and as I passed through the magnificent iron gates at the entrance to the estate, past the artificial lakes and its hungry ducks, I took my farewell of the Holy Hill and Mormond Tam and touched my cap to Lady Cauldock, who had cared little for the place. The road ahead was wide and free — and I was off to the Lands of Whig-About.

The Lands of Whig-About can be found three miles east of Strichen. I had never heard the name before, and I doubt if many other people have, for you will never find it on any map, yet what went on there two centuries ago was enough to make honest folk lie awake in their beds. It was a nest of thieves and poachers, a hiding place for smugglers, and at its lowest ebb it was condemned as 'a city of sin and misery'.

Yet, things could have been so different. It was here in the Lands of Whig-About that the Frasers planned another 'new town'. Their aim was to call it New Leeds, for it was to rival the great industrial town of Leeds in Yorkshire. The man behind the scheme was Lord Strichen's son, Captain Alexander Fraser, of the Dragoon Guards, who acted as guide to Boswell and Johnson when they visited the Strichen Stone Circle. Boswell described him as 'the worthy son of a worthy father, the late Lord Strichen', but events at New Leeds proved him anything but that.

There was a fair at Strichen during Boswell and Johnson's visit and Captain Fraser invited several people from it to meet his guests at dinner. The Captain seems to have taken a boyish delight in fairs; he ran a number of them to boost his plans for New Leeds. His father had offered a premium to the man who had the first 'reekin' lum' in Strichen, but Captain Fraser had more unusual ideas for capturing public interest in *his* new town. He offered a prize to commemorate the first fair in 1799 — a prize for 'the drunkest man that should appear at the market'. The winner, who was a weaver and a joiner, won an eight-day clock.

Unlike other new towns that spread and prospered across Buchan, New Leeds never made it. In 1858, Dr Pratt described it in his book, *Buchan*, as 'the straggling and miserable-looking village of New Leeds'. Another account of it in 1875 said it was 'a poor place with only eighteen dwelling-houses'. As well as being a haunt of poachers and smugglers, it was the home of some wonderful eccentrics like the local joiner, who took up residence in a ruined byre and slept in a coffin. Whether this was the drunken joiner who won Captain Fraser's eight-day clock is not recorded. In later years, New Leeds residents were reported to have given up lawless pursuits and turned to honest labour, but it was never to rise from the ashes of its own vice and indolence. While it slipped into obscurity, Captain Fraser went off to lay out the White Horse of Mormond Hill, commemorating the time when his white charger was shot from under him.

If it was 'a city of sin and misery', Christian Watt blamed most of the misery on the Frasers of Strichen. In one memorable clash with the habbering Laird she attacked him for getting Capability Brown to lay-out a beautiful park around Strichen House while ignoring the needs of the 'new town' residents. 'You did not get him to lay out New Leeds', she said. 'Some of the first inhabitants are living in shacks and tattie boxes. You had dreams of huge spinning factories rising in Buchan, not, as you say, to give work to the poor, but to further your own wealth and interest'.

Today, there are no shacks and tattie boxes in New Leeds, which hides away from the world just off the Aberdeen-Fraserburgh road, but it is still something of a straggling village. The bad old days are recalled by the street names — Lovat Road, for instance, after Mormond Tam. Jim Scott, who lives at 29 Manse Street, told me that he had the wrong address — it should be 29 New Leeds, for when his house was built there were no streets.

'Come and see this', he said, and dug out the deeds of his house, which carried a reference to 'a Portion of Land No. 29'. The document referred to 'the piece of ground sometime belonging to Alexander Fraser, Esquire of Strichen and of that part of the Lands of Strichen in the parish of Buchan and county of Aberdeen'. The ground, it said, 'was proposed to be feud out for raising a village to be called the village of Leeds, now called New Leeds'.

'Read that', said Jim, and his finger pointed to a line which said that the Lands of Strichen 'were formerly called the Town and Lands of Whig-About'. He had no idea what the name meant, and I have never been able to trace its origin. The only clue I could find was an entry in William M. Alexander's *Place-Names of Aberdeenshire*, which read 'Whigabutts'. Alexander said that the Monymusk Papers spoke about 'whigg about riggs', but added that the term was unexplained.

The walls of Jim Scott's house came from local sources, including quartz stones from the Hill of Mormond. It was a thackit hoosie at one time. Jim's parents had a croft called Village Lands, but his mother didn't like the name and changed it to Holmlea. Part of the ground was also the market stance and tinkers were entitled to use it when it wasn't in crop. They had to use the land every three years or they lost the right to it.

New Leeds has become Old Leeds and not many people know or care about Mormond Tam, Lady Cauldock and the Frasers of Strichen. The only positive reminder is the White Horse of Mormond, which has become a landmark as well-known as the Holy Hill itself.

CHAPTER SEVEN

Causeways of Kininmonth

The Muckle Causeway of Kininmonth carried travellers across the boggy acres of Buchan in the days when the Comyn Earls of Buchan held power in the North-east. The causeway, which was said to lie along the line of a primeval track used by the Picts for more than a thousand years, came into being when a stronghold was built at Rattray to guard the tidal inlet at the mouth of the Loch of Strathbeg.

This was the Comyns' principal port, but when they looked landward they were cut off from the heart of the country by swamps and mosses, so they paved the old track and constructed a causeway 'running over morasses and wastes, past a gloomy loch, towards the south-west'. There were, in fact, two causeways or 'cassies', the Muckle and the Little Causeway of Kininmonth, and together they formed what was probably the first piece of major road-building in the North.

The line was roughly from Crimond to Old Deer and the route can be pinpointed more accurately by the 'gloomy loch', which was the Loch of Kininmonth, and by Corse Farm and Corsend, a little to the south. 'The Cross' is marked on old maps, and the Causeway was also known as the Corse or Cross of Kininmonth, which meant a crossing over a water-shed.

Treading ancient trails as I headed north to the Loch of Strathbeg, I took guidance from a description of the old Causey which I had seen in a document written in 1722, dealing with the parish of Lonmay. It read: 'Half a mile to the east of Kininmonth ther is the remains of an old chappell and a burial-place, though now in desuetude. The king's high way

59

goeth from Inveralochie, south by the church to the calsay of Kininmonth, being through a moss, one mile to the west of the house of Kininmonth; near to which causay, on the north side, ther's the Loch of Kininmunth, which will be two miles in circumference, but produceth no kind of fish'.

The farms on the road to Crimond had names that were reminders of the old Causeway — Corsend and Corse Farm — and farther on others seemed to point the way to the Loch of Kininmonth. Lochills was on my left, Loch Croft and Loch Cottage on my right, but there was no sign of the loch itself and nobody seemed to know where it was or where it had been. Then I met Bill Allan, from Corse Farm, who remembered seeing it as a boy on Lochills Farm. Rushes from it had been used to make thatch for thackit hoosies, but at the end of the last war a ditch was dug by POWs and the loch was drained.

It must have been a dreary out-of-the-world corner of the North-east when the Comyns held Buchan in thrall. Even today, so many centuries later, it still seems a remote and lonely place when you see the peaty acres of the great Mosses of Rora and St Fergus spreading across the landscape. Not much more than a mile south-east of Loch Farm is the ruined Kirk of Kininmonth, with a bird-cage bellcote on the south gable and underneath it a faded clock gifted to the church in 1930. Beyond it, great peat stacks can be seen rising at Blackhills on the edge of the St Fergus moss.

Here, where crofters once cut peat with their flaughter-spades, machines from Herbst Peat and Energy (Scotland) now cut it commercially to send to Sweden, where, oddly enough, it is used for central heating. Michael Herbst is a German who came to Scotland from Ireland, where he had been making peat-cutting machinery. He now has 1100 acres of land and two farms in Buchan — 460 acres at the St Fergus moss and 300 at the Rora moss.

The St Fergus moss rubs shoulders with Rora and all around are farms and crofts that defied the black suffocation of peat. They have names like Moss-side, Boghead, Mosstown and, a curious one this, Mossgirl. I never found out what lay behind *that* name, but all are pointers to why the Muckle Causeway of Kininmonth had to be built.

I pressed on, following what was roughly the line of the 'king's highway that goeth to Inveralochie', keeping an eye open for a croft which Bill Allan had mentioned. It stood on a brae not far from the Crimond road. There was no name outside it but John Cannon, the occupant, confirmed it — it was Causewayhill, or, as Bill Allan had said, Cassiehill. Here on this back road was what was probably the only remaining link with the ancient Causeway of Kininmonth.

From there I went on through Crimond, whose church clock has a curious 61 minutes to the hour. Two miles up the road was Lonmay, where an uncle of mine had a souter's shop before the war. Between Crimond and the Loch of Strathbeg was the farm I was looking for — Starnafin. The name is thought to come from *stairean*, meaning stepping stones, and *fionn*, white.

Starnafin is the visitor centre for the RSPB's reserve at the Loch of Strathbeg. Here, where a couple of enthusiastic bird-watchers had binoculars glued to their eyes, a notice board carried the mind-boggling information that 52,700 pinkfeet geese were roosting on the loch, not to mention a consider-able number of greylag and barnacle geese, pochards, whooper swans, teal, mallard, shovellers and others. There are four hides on the edge of the loch, but when I went down to one of them the birds — or, at any rate, the geese — had flown.

It was all so different the first time I was there. That was seven or eight years ago, when I drove to Crimond in the dark to meet Jim Dunbar, the warden, at six-thirty in the morning so that I could see the geese take-off on their flight to the feed-ing grounds. A half-moon lit our way through the old Crimond airfield, still in use as a Royal Navy radio station, to the hides. I was told that when there was a half-moon or a full moon the geese would linger in the fields and eat in darkness, sometimes staying away for two or three days and nights.

Dawn broke, spreading a grey finger of light across the sky, and I watched, puzzled, as geese repeatedly rose, flapping their wings, and dropped down again on to the loch, almost as if they were unable to make up their minds to go or to stay, to soar away towards that bright yellow moon or to settle down on the water for another forty winks. But that was how they did it, looking for contact with the others, for signs that the time was right. If the rest of the flock made no movement then the early fliers settled on the water and waited. The swans did it another way. One swan would nod its head up and down, but if no other swan did the same the nodding stopped. When one swan after another began to nod they were ready for flight.

I still remember the incredible moment of take-off ... a tidal wave of pinkfeet moving across the loch, getting the wind under their wings, lifting from the water in a sudden rush, thousands of them, the sound of their wings merging into a great roar in the dawn sky. I remember, too, Jim Buchan telling me that it never failed to excite him — it was the mystery of it all. 'Geese and Buchan go together', he said. 'I've seen them down on the edge of the Wash and it looks far too civilised. But here you see a wild Buchan sky; you know, one of those windy, wild skies, and the geese coming in during the winter. It all fits in'.

I left Starnafin and made my way along the coast, passing the forbidding ruins of Inverallochy Castle. The castle was a Comyn stronghold, as was Cairnbulg Castle, less than two miles away. Cairnbulg was restored and became the home of the Frasers of Philorth, now represented by Baroness Saltoun, wife of Captain Alexander Ramsay of Mar. Inverallochy Castle fared less well. It stood by the Loch of Inverallochy, but the loch has gone and all that is left of the castle is the stump of a tower. It was a Fraser of Philorth who built Kinnaird Castle, which was where I was heading.

A cadet branch of the Comyns was established at Inverallochy by Jordanus de Cummin and there is a questionable tale about a stone being found in the old castle with the inscription on it:

I Jurdan Cuming, indweller here,
Gat this hous and lands for biggin the Abbey of Deer.

The coastline between Peterhead and Fraserburgh, spectac-
ularly beautiful despite its raw winds and drizzling rain, carries the imprint of history at almost every step of the way. The
fisher poet, Peter Buchan, once took me on a nostalgic stroll
down to Buchanhaven by the Ware Road in Peterhead, where
farmers came with their carts to collect *ware* (seaweed) for fer-
tiliser. In *Buchanhaven Shorie* he wrote about old men sitting
by a garden dyke on a seat that

Looks oot owre the pier an' the half-sunk rocks
Wi' their skirts o' dark-broon weed,
To the bonny sweep o' yalla san'
An' the licht at Rattray Heid.

Peter was the voice of the Blue Toon, while John C. Milne
breathed magic into the Doric and spoke in his own inim-
itable way for the Broch:

O Tam, gie me auld Faithlie toon
Whar trees are scrunts for miles aroon
And nae a burn wad slake or droon
A drunken miller.

As I made my way along the coast to Fraserburgh Bay I was
thinking of the two towns and their ancient rivalry. Peterhead
has always seemed to be one jump ahead. It built itself into a
major fishing port and when oil — 'black gold' — came along
the Blue Mogganers cashed in on that. Even in the great days
of whaling, when the hunt was on for a different kind of oil,
whale oil, Peterhead, with some thirty whalers in the Arctic,
was well ahead of Fraserburgh.

The Brochers, however, have always gone their own way —
they 'gang their ain gait', as J. C. Milne said of Buchan folk
generally, 'wi' a lach or a spit or a sweir'. I like the story of
how they kept their end up when Peterhead was making a

name for itself during the whaling years. 'Half of our whaling fleet sailed yesterday', proclaimed a notice at the harbour. 'The other half will leave tomorrow'. What it didn't say was that half of the fleet was one ship — there were only two whalers sailing from the port.

In the distance I could see Kinnaird Head Lighthouse, which has become automatic. A new national lighthouse museum has been established at Kinnaird Head and, although the old light has gone, half a dozen new lights have replaced it. They shine out *inside* the museum — lights from Sanda in the Mull of Kintyre, Rinnes in Islay, Dunnet Head, the Fair Isle, Niest Point in Sky and Turnberry. The lenses from these were dismantled, taken to Fraserburgh, and put together *inside* the new museum.

Jim Oliver, who was principal lighthouse keeper at Kinnaird Head before it was automated, was responsible for putting the huge lenses together again. 'Heavy, heavy stuff', he said. There were 6 tons of glass on top of the Sanda plinth, $3^1/_2$ tons on Niest Point, 4 tons on Fair Isle. But he had special interest in the lights. His father, Robert Oliver, was a lighthouse keeper and served on three of them — Niest Point, Dunnet Head and Sanda. The lights provide a spectacular display inside the museum.

Jim once showed me a visitors' book going back to June, 1894, when the Kinnaird Head Lighthouse was opened. The first entries were from a large party from Peterhead, there to see what the Brochers were up to. Before the museum opened, I asked Jim Oliver if he thought that the Blue Mogganers would head the queue again. 'They'll be here first to see if they're being upstaged', he said.

The most notable feature in the museum is the huge viewing window in the restaurant. Below it I could see what looked like a mini-lighthouse — the new automatic light. 'That's what we've come to', said Jim. 'That's progress'. It seemed woefully inadequate beside the old lighthouse. 'It'll be all right once it grows up', joked Jim. The rocks below wore Peter Buchan's 'skirts o' dark broon weed' and stretching away beyond them was the limitless ocean. 'When you stand here you could be anywhere in the world', said Jim. 'There are no bounds. You get the maximum horizon'.

Kinnaird Head, sticking out into the sea like a knotted fist, gave Fraserburgh a lead over Peterhead in the great days of the herring fishing. Because of its position, it was said that the herring shoals passed along the coast 'hugging the shore' where the strongest tides ran, so that only the strongest and best fish were able to make head against them. The result was that herring caught at Fraserburgh were among the best sent to market. The years between 1870 and 1900 were the most prosperous for the Broch fishermen. In 1820 the port had fewer than 120 boats at the fishing, and in 1872 it had 626.

From the museum restaurant I could see a line of houses huddled on the shore where the coastline curved round a point called Clubbie Craig. 'That's Broadsea', said Jim. There was a tenuous link between Broadsea and the old lighthouse. Christian Watt, the servant girl who became the scourge of the Buchan lairds (see Chapter 6), was born in Broadsea. Her great-grandfather was William Lascelles, the last Hereditary Constable of Broadsea, whose wife, Jane Crawford, was the illegitimate daughter of Jean Crawford and John Gordon of Kinellar. The Gordons were the last to live in Kinnaird Head Castle before it was turned into a lighthouse.

Broadsea has been swallowed up by the Broch, and many of the old fisher houses — the two-roomed 'but and bens' — have been heightened and modernised. Yet 'Bredsie', as they call it, still retains something of the character of the old Seatoun. Jim Coull, whose house at 28 Broadsea is its original size, said that at one time every house in the village was a 'but and ben'. Some have no doors opening on to the street. This is because the houses were made with the doors facing the sea.

Neat drying greens run along the shore in front of the houses. In winter, the waves reach out almost to their doorsteps, spraying white spume over slanting rocks that lie across each other like slates on a rooftop. That's what the old fishermen call the rocks, said Jim — the Slates. Round the bay was the Gwight or Gyte, a cleft in the rocks. It is a common name along the Buchan coast.

Christian Watt was born at 72 Broadsea in 1833. Sixty-three years later, her grand-daughter, Christian Watt Marshall, was born in the same house. She not only inherited her grand-mother's sharp eye and sharp tongue, but also her talent for writing, for at the age of eighty-three she began to write a book about Broadsea and the Broch. She called it *A Stranger on the Bars* and when it was completed she was eighty-nine.

In her book, she described her 'little house', which was built in the 17th century and had changed little through the years:

Like all the houses in Broadsea it was a typical fisher's cottage with a large central closet and a box bed at each end. Near the kitchen fireplace the floor was laid with Caithness flagstones — the rest was beaten earth, freshly sanded every day. The but end had a wooden floor, plastered walls with a dado rail all round and a varnished boarded ceiling. The ben had open rafter beams with boards laid across them to hold the fishing gear. The warmth of the house kept the nets and lines dry. The kitchen fireplace was an old hanging lum with a wooden canopy similar to a blacksmith's forge. Inside it there were tenter sticks for smoking fish and hams. Fishers sometimes kept a pig for curing, but that was before my time. Those wooden lums were danger-ous brutes, they could catch fire so easily.

You can see from the outside walls that the house has twice been heightened. Two layers of stone were added in 1910 and it was heightened again in 1920. Here, too, a small window — the closet window, little more than a foot square — has been blocked up. No. 72 was neat, clean and tidy — inside and out. Christian Watt Marshall would have approved, for she said that to be dirty or 'throwither' was an unpardonable sin. She wrote of one family who lived in an outhouse, yet their 'brass-es always shone like dollars'.

When I was inside the house, surrounded by old paintings,

family photographs, cabinets full of beautiful china and magnificent furniture, I was thinking of the two Christians whose lives had started at 72 Broadsea. Here, the first Christian had met her sweetheart, home from the whaling, and had married him 'in the middle of the floor in the ben' in December, 1858. Here, too, the second Christian — Christian Watt Marshall — had sat by the fire as a child mending her father's fishing nets by the light of a paraffin lamp.

I was keeping company with the past. I could almost see the faces and hear the 'Bredsie' voices drifting down the years. Christian Watt's portrait looked down on me from a wall at the 'but' end of the house, along with those of her mother and father. Through in the 'ben' there was a large oil painting of ruined Cairnbulg Castle before it was restored, and out in the lobby was another painting of old Broadsea village, with peat smoke curling from a lum. At one time, salted fish would have lain on its red roof, drying in the sun. It was this painting that was used as the front cover of A *Stranger on the Bars*.

I left the 'little house' and its memories and went west, passing Dr Pratt's 'good and safe harbour' at Sandhaven, now crumbling into the sea, and little Pittulie, which the doctor said contained 'nothing particularly worth of notice'. It seemed still and deserted when I was there, and it had grown a little shabby. Odd to think that this tiny village once had forty-six boats, while between them Pittulie and Broadsea had 170 men at the fishing.

I was looking for the Court Road, for I was heading for Boyndlie on my way to Banff. 'Every Sunday morning', wrote Christian Watt Marshall, 'the Laird and his Lady, the Ogilvy Forbes from Boyndlie, came down the Court Road in a landau driven by two white horses, bound for the Catholic chapel in the Broch'. It reminded me of another youngster who had watched the laird, John Charles Mathias Ogilvie-Forbes, riding past on his way to church. Roy Skinner, whose father was born at Boyndlie and had a carpenter's shop on the estate, often watched the laird's carriage leaving the estate by the lodge and passing close to his house. Ogilvie-Forbes had a beard and resembled King Edward VI.

Roy, who had a memory as sharp as a pin even when he was into his nineties, was a chartered engineer and served part of his apprenticeship in the boatbuilding yard of J. & G. Forbes in Sandhaven, where in those far-off days they built magnificent yachts with names like Maender, Wayfarer, Cramond Brig and Auld Reekie.

I always called Roy the Skinner loon. He was the Grand Old Man of the Buchan Heritage Society and a devotee of J. C. Milne. He went to the same school at Memsie and for a number of years, even when he was into his nineties, he travelled around Buchan talking to clubs and societies about Milne and his poetry. Some years ago I sent him a birthday card with a Doric verse in the style of J. C. Milne. After that he insisted that I should always mark his birthdays in this way. The last one, with apologies to Milne, was written in 1994:

As I gaed doon by Memsie
I heard an aul' man speir,
'Faur's the bonnie dialect
That aince wis spoken here?'

Faur's the birn o' bairnies
That cam tae Memsie skweel
Fae smiddy, craft and fairm
And cottar-hoose as weel?

Ach, weel, I heard the aul' man say,
It's nae the same place noo,
Gweed sakes, it's nae surprisin'
For, dyod, I'm ninety-two.

I telt the aul' man nae tae fash,
Yer the Skinner loon tae me,
Ye'll plough a lang, lang furrow yet,
So gyaung on tae ninety-three!

In March, 1995, Roy was taken to hospital with a stroke. I sat at his bedside and we spoke about the old days. He began to recite a verse of Milne's poetry and there were tears in his eyes. Two months after going home from convalescence he went into a private nursing home at Auquharney in Hatton, only a short distance from Auchleuchries, where my grandfather had his croft all those years ago. He died there on November 5, 1995, less than a month after reaching his ninety-third birthday. He was buried in the little kirkyard at Tarves, where his parents had been laid to rest. It was there that I said my last farewell to the Skinner loon.

CHAPTER EIGHT

Cairness and Crimonmogate

Looking across the flat farmlands of Buchan from the House of Cairness the Hill of Mormond can be seen rising above the surrounding countryside with a raggety coxcomb of communication masts on its head. It is a view that Phillip Miller, an architectural historian from Bedfordshire, sees every day from his bedroom on the first floor of his 18th century mansion house near St Combs. When he bought Cairness in the autumn of 1994 he knew little about Mormond and its White Horse — and even less about Buchan. 'I'd never even *heard* of Buchan', he told me. He had only once been in Aberdeen — and the only stately home he had seen in the North-east was Duff House at Banff, which he visited sixteen years ago.

Nevertheless, he knew all about the magnificent Georgian mansion hidden away in what was to him a remote and little-known corner of North-east Scotland. When he was studying architecture he had a special interest in the Cairness period, the 1790s. He knew, too, about the architect who had designed the house, James Playfair, who died before the work was completed. If he had lived, said Miller, Playfair would have been Scotland's greatest architect. Playfair's widow called in another man to finish the job — the English architect John (later Sir John) Sloane, who was Miller's idol and 'a great hero to all young architects'.

In those formative years of Phillip Miller's career he could never have imagined that *he* would one day be the Laird of Cairness. It came about quite by chance. When he was carrying out restoration work on 18th century Ampthill Park in Bedfordshire he went on a train journey and bought a country magazine to pass the time. In it was an advertisement that changed his life. 'There it was', he recalls, 'this house which I'd known, advertised for sale at a price which in the south would seem like peanuts'. Cairness was on the market for £170,000 — and Phillip and his wife Pat, an interior decorator, made up their minds to bid for it. They would sell up, move north to Buchan, and still have money left over to restore it to its former glory.

It promised to be a herculean task. For a start, there were forty-two rooms in the house — that, at any rate, is what Phillip thought; he never got around to counting them. There were eight main bedrooms, five bathrooms, and nine secondary bedrooms, while at the rear of the house was a huge semicircular court of buildings and offices, a bell tower, and an ice house. There were also fifty-two cast-iron chimneys, each one a Doric column about 6ft. high and so heavy that not even two men could lift it. Pat Miller said that her husband lay awake at night worrying about one of them breaking off and crashing down on the house.

But the Millers are remarkably relaxed about the task that faces them. They have worked it out that they can stabilise the building for around £50,000 by carrying out much of the work themselves, helped by local tradesmen. After the building has been stabilised, they can take their time over the restoration work. They plan to hold seminars and concerts at Cairness and their long-term aim is to turn the house into a private museum, using as a basis for it their own collections of old clocks, 18th and 19th century teapots and coffee pots, and musical instruments.

Cairness House, built in 1791–97 at a cost of about £25,000, was designed by James Playfair for Charles Gordon of Buthlaw. The mansion, once described as one of the wonders of Buchan, is tarnished a little by the years, but still carrying reminders of the grace and elegance that made it the finest neo-classical mansion in Scotland. You can understand why, seeing it for the first time, the Millers thought it 'absolutely fantastic', better than anything they had expected. Phillip Miller told me about his plans for the house as we sat in the

Business Room. Out of the window we could see one of the 'blind' arches that marks the end of the Court of Offices, which forms a massive semi-circle at the rear of the house. It is entered through an archway capped by a cupola. Playfair's preoccupation with arches, circles and diamonds could be seen all over the house, on the ceilings, on the doors, on the walls.

Walking through some of the forty-two rooms was like slipping in and out of the past. From an ornate frieze in the dining room Bacchus, god of wine and giver of ecstasy, looked down on a long table laid out with exquisite taste, almost as if a large dinner party had been expected that evening. The Ladies Room, or Morning Room, housed a piano dating from 1785, some five years before the house was built. Here, in its original state, the domed ceiling would have been decorated with a blue sky and clouds, while in the library a night sky with stars would have covered the ceiling. 'We'll do that eventually', said Phillip. Pat, who is an interior designer, will take care of it.

The head of Apollo, god of poetry and music, formed part of the frieze in the music room, along with a series of lyres. The Millers followed the lyre theme by putting a harp into the room. At the opposite end of the room was another period piece, a second piano, early 19th century. It is in this room that the Millers plan to hold their concerts, the visitors sitting on antique chairs, not as a formal audience, but scattered about in a more relaxed way.

The first of these concerts and seminars were actually held at Cairness before Phillip Miller had seriously begun the work of restoration. There was dry rot upstairs, and bare rooms still to be tackled, but he went ahead with a seminar on English china. There was a small invited audience, among them two people travelling up from the Midlands, three from Edinburgh. They plan to build on this, but they have no intention of creating a second Haddo House in Buchan.

A number of wind instruments lay on top of the piano and also a book of music dated 1814, the year before the piano was made. It was entitled 'A Selection of Original Scottish

Airs' and it lay open at 'O Logie of Buchan'. I could almost hear the music and words of the old ballad come drifting up through the centuries in that quiet, pleasant room. All that was needed to complete the picture was the viol:

O Logie o' Buchan, O Logie the laird,
They hae ta'en awa' Jamie that delv'd in the yard,
Wha play'd on the pipe an' the viol sae sma,
They hae ta'en awa Jamie the flower o' them a'.

The best-known room in the house is the Egyptian Room with its hieroglyphic friezes. Playfair had produced interesting symbols, but they didn't mean anything. It was all done before anyone had translated Egyptian hieroglyphics, so Playfair made up his own. Above the door was a large inscription on wood reading, 'And the Whole was Completed July MDCCXCVII, James Playfair Aberdeen'. This, it is thought, was put up at the centenary of the house.

The Egyptian Room was the Billiard Room and inside a cupboard was a small billiard table. It wasn't a period piece. They couldn't get one of the right vintage so they settled for a later model — at least temporarily.

So we wandered through the old house, upstairs to a long, beautiful corridor where every bedroom had its dressing room, peeking into a bathroom where a magnificent white bath held pride of place, sneaking a look at a magnificent four-poster bed in one of the rooms — the first bedroom in the house to be decorated. Then down to the semi-circular courtyard, whose buildings had housed the laundry, dairy, offices and servants' quarters. Inside the ice-house, which dropped 20ft. underground, there was a circular passage which had been the larder, with hooks still hanging from the ceiling. The bell in the tower above the ice-house was used to call workers in from the fields.

Phillip Miller, small, delicately whiskered, quietly spoken, is a happy convert to Buchan. Friends who have come up from the south have fallen in love with it. 'It's not been spoiled by tourists', he said. 'We should all be quiet about it'. Pat, slim, friendly, busy, is no Lady Cauldock. The only thing that worried her about the weather was that she couldn't get the grass cut. I saw her come up the steps of the porch laden with shopping and half-expected to see the butler hurry out to help her — or, perhaps, John the Turk.

Charles Gordon's son, Major-General Thomas Gordon, rose to high rank in the Royal Greek Army, defeated the Turks, and wrote a history of the Greek Revolution. His wife was Armenian. When he returned to Cairness after the Greek War of Independence, the General took with him his faithful Armenian batman, John Turk. Like his master, he spent the rest of his days in Buchan 'smoking in glorious ease'. In his old age he wanted to go home to his own people, but he died on his way to Greece.

He was a familiar figure all over Buchan, riding around on a mule or a horse. Christian Watt, in her memoirs, recalled seeing the 'dark-skinned Armenian who used to come into the Broch on a white horse'. He lived in a chaumer at Cairness and was 'an imposing figure in a turban and red cloak'. Phillip Miller had heard people talk about Johnny the Turk, but he was surprised to learn that at one time there was a full-sized portrait of him among the paintings in the House of Cairness. It was said that it was a faithful likeness of John, 'a handsome fellow in picturesque native costume and armour'. Wherever it is now, no one would be more delighted than Phillip Miller to see it back in Cairness.

Before I left Cairness we stood and chatted on the porch which had been designed by John Sloane, looking across the fields to the Hill of Mormond. Dr John Pratt thought that the porch was 'exceedingly chaste'. The granite for its Ionic columns came from the Cairngall quarries at Longside. On the left was the long drive, running between trees from the entrance gate, set between two small lodges, with gate piers guarded by two sphinxes — again, the Egyptian touch. Like the inscription inside the Egyptian room, the sphinxes were put there at the time of the centenary.

Unlike many Buchan mansions, Cairness is not hemmed in by trees — Dr John Pratt described it as a 'most notable and *conspicuous* object to the surrounding country' — but not much more than a mile away another great Buchan house hides away in the woods of Crimonmogate. When Phillip Miller came to Buchan he thought it a marvellous place for fine mansion houses, but he had no idea that he would be near-neighbour to one of the most impressive of them.

Crimonmogate House was the work of Archibald Simpson. It was built in 1825, five years after Simpson's Assembly Rooms in Aberdeen (later incorporating the Music Hall) were completed. In this quiet Buchan backwater Simpson, the up and coming architectural genius from Aberdeen, duplicated the six huge Ionic columns of the Music Hall. The house was built by Sir Charles Bannerman, who employed Simpson to plan not only the New House of Crimonmogate, replacing a late-17th century mansion, but also a large number of smaller buildings on the estate, among them the West Lodge, with its proto-Doric portico.

The Logie Lodges were also Simpson's work. These twin gate lodges led to Logie, once a Gordon lairdship, acquired by Sir Charles in the middle of the 19th century. This was the setting for the famous ballad, which is said to have been written by George Halket, who taught at Rathen. The hero 'Jamie' was the gardener at Logie, while the heroine was Isobel Keith, who later married a well-to-do farmer, William Keith, from Tyacksnook. She died in 1826 at the age of eighty-nine. I have often wondered if, sitting on her 'creepie' in her old age, she still had the half-sixpence that Jamie gave her when her 'daddy' and 'minny' (mother) broke up the romance:

I sit on my creepie and spin at my wheel,
And think on the laddie that lo'ed me sae weel,
He had but ae saxpence, he brak it in twa,
And ga'ed me the hauf o't when he ga'ed awa.

When Sir Charles died in 1851 he was succeeded by Sir

Alexander Bannerman, M.P. for Aberdeenshire and a well-known public figure. The estate eventually came into the hands of Sir Alexander's great-grandson, Major R. A. Carnegie, but in 1991–92 he handed it over to his son, the Hon. Jocelyn Carnegie. Major Carnegie was better known to the public as Sacha Carnegie, the novelist. His real first name is Raymond; the Sacha was adopted as a pen-name because his mother was Polish. He is still writing. When I was at Crimonmogate he was working on a number of projects, including film scripts, and was finishing another novel. Back in 1958 he wrote a book called *Pigs I have Known*, a hilarious account of his attempt to set up a piggery at Crimonmogate. This is how he saw Buchan, crowned by little Mormond Hill and its white stone horse, a land of great winds, sturdy people, curlews, kestrels and hoodie-craws:

Buchan is a land of farmers and fishermen; of the geese and the great winds: 'The little land, withdrawn beyond the hills and flanked with friendless seas'.

The sea surrounds it on three sides, north, north-east and east, and to the east lies Norway (some three hundred miles from the piggery to Stavanger).

This is not the romantic Scotland of mountains and mist and heathery postcards, but rather a flat land — some might be tempted to call it bleak — sparsely graced with trees and open to every breeze. We only possess one hill, rising rounded and gentle to eight hundred feet, a hill visible for miles; covered with heather and decorated with a white stone stag and a white stone horse.

Grouse live there and on the many small peat mosses dotted below on the flat; and the birds of solitude, the curlew, the kestrel and the hoodie-crow. On clear days it is possible to see the mountains of Western Aberdeenshire with the spike of Benachie thrusting into the distant sky.

But the inhabitants of Buchan are not Highlandmen; they are a race unto themselves, unlike any throughout the rest of Scotland, a race as sturdy, hardy, solid and unbending as the granite of their earth, speaking in tones and using words very reminiscent of Scandinavia and the Friesian coast. This is not surprising considering that the Norsemen came raiding their longships every day.

During his time at Crimonmogate, Major Carnegie was responsible for a good deal of restoration and renovation work on the estate. Jocelyn Carnegie and his wife, Susie, carried on the tradition, doing on a small scale what the Millers were doing on a more intimidating scale at Cairness . . . getting the house back to its original state. The difference was that Crimonmogate had been lived in. Many of the large rooms were divided into smaller rooms by previous occupiers and the Carnegies set about removing all the partitions, bringing back space and a sense of what it was like in the old days.

Crimonmogate runs to 1,400 acres, including two main farms, but it is small compared to what it once was. Its original size can be seen on a map of the estate, about 6ft. long, which hangs on one of the stairway walls. Dated 1776, it was drawn before the house was built. There are two lochs on the estate. The oldest is Crimonmogate Loch, which was laid out in 1860; the other is the Loch of Logie, which was dug out in 1991–92 and stocked with trout. The Logie loch, which is called the Fishery, is now leased out.

Not far from a gate leading to the Fishery a road goes off to Savoch, which reminded me of the time they were *draining* lochs in this area, not filling them in. At Strathbeg, Nature created one of the biggest lochs in Buchan, but at the end of the 18th century one man tried to undo its work. Maps show a windmill near the edge of the loch. This was the Savoch windpump, built about 1791 by a Mr Sellar, who planned to use it to drain the loch. Thousands of pounds were spent on the project, but it was a complete failure.

Susie Carnegie showed me round the house. The hall is magnificent, tall, fluted columns leading up to a cornice and a coffered ceiling with a glazed dome at the centre. Through the drawing room and the dining room, with its striking family portraits . . . the well-stocked library ('He loves books',

Susie said of her father-in-law) . . . and the billiard room, the table set for play. Upstairs there were antlers and stuffed ducks in the gunroom and in the corridor we looked down on the dome above the hall. Then down to the basement, where we tramped through what, like Cairness, seemed to be an interminable network of corridors, finally landing back where we started.

They still had the octagonal dairy, built in 1825, which they planned to restore as a game larder, and the obelisk erected by Charles Bannerman in 1821 to the memory of Patrick Milne. Milne, the son of Alexander Milne, an Aberdeen merchant, who purchased the estate in the late 18th century, succeeded to the estate in 1800 and later bequeathed it to Charles Bannerman. On the lawn in front of the house is an 18th century sundial decorated with Prince of Wales feathers.

Crimonmogate seemed well ahead of Cairness in the restoration stakes. Both Phillip Miller and Jocelyn Carnegie, who runs a business which operates from Cumbria, had the same aim in mind . . . to recapture the grandeur of two of Buchan's finest stately homes. The future of Crimonmogate certainly seemed to be in safe hands. When I was talking to Susie Carnegie, four-year-old Merlin Carnegie, who would one day be Laird of this great Buchan estate, reached into his pocket, banged down a handful of coins on the table, and announced, 'I'm getting rich!' A few weeks later I learned that Crimonmogate was up for sale.

CHAPTER NINE

Under the Waggle

The village of Cuminestown straggles along the edge of a long flat ridge of land known as Waggle Hill. Local people call it simply the Waggle, a name that comes from an old Scots meaning 'a quaking bog'. In this corner of Monquhitter, on the western rim of Buchan, the farms are identified in the same uncompromising way . . . Bogenlea, Blackbog, Meikle-bog, Rush-head, Rashypans; it sometimes seems as if the whole of Buchan had grown out of one great peat bog.

In the late 18th and early 19th centuries the countryside was mostly 'moss and moor, full of bogies and marshes', and it was in this barren territory that Buchan's 'new towns' were born. It was the age of the Improvers, when the lairds set out to tame the land, reclaiming it from the marshes, establishing new villages, feuing pockets of land to settlers at modest rents, encouraging weavers to work at their trade.

'The whole world changed', wrote Christian Watt, 'not gradually, but suddenly, like lightning. Gangs of men came in to reclaim the land, ploughing bogs and stanks. Suddenly huge big packs were marching up the side of Mormond Hill, so greedy did they become for land'.*

It was Waggle Hill, not Mormond, that claimed most attention in the early days, for it was here that Buchan's first 'new town' took shape. The official jargon of the time described the development as the 'planting' of villages. In the aftermath of the '45 Jacobite Rising, the Inspectors of Forfeited Estates had declared that 'nothing was more likely to civilise the inhabitants of upland Aberdeenshire and Banffshire than the

*The Christian Watt Papers.

79

plantation of villages, all with linen works, post-offices, market and prison'.

Now the civilising of Buchan had come a step nearer with the building of Cuminestown. Completed in 1763, it took its name from its founder, Joseph Cumine of Auchry, who had as his adviser Sir Archibald Grant of Archieston, one of the leading improvers of his day. He told Cumine that a 'new town' was the only way to improve his land 'with certain profit'. Cumine was both a practical man and a visionary. He knew what the future held, and he knew, too, the worth of the moorland farm that stood on the site he had selected for development. It yielded only the paltry sum of £11 a year.

His neighbours thought him mad and mocked him, believing that his scheme was impracticable, but before long settlers began to flock to Cuminestown. 'Soon there were seventy-five feus occupied by a set of industrious, honest and active feuars', it was reported. The laird made sure that they remained industrious and honest by checking on their progress. He held regular meetings with them in a local inn and rewarded them with a glass of whisky. He made them keep a book of worthwhile improvements and commended those who carried them out.

The hard workers got a dram, the slackers got short shrift. 'All who do not improve', it was reported, 'are debarred and go by the name of drones'. There were, at any rate, no drones in the settlers homes, for linen was spun by every family and '1000 pairs of cargo hose at 1/– per pair are annually sent to market'. But some 'improving' lairds liked to show that they were interested in culture as well as cash. Lord Strichen, whose planned village appeared a year after Cuminestown, said it was intended to promote the *arts* as well as 'the manufactures of this country'. Cuminestown, however, was first in the field, and it could also claim that it had produced the new towns' first poet.

William Ingram was born in the village in 1765, two years after it came into being. He became a weaver in a weavers' town, doing farm work to augment his income, but in his spare time he studied to become a teacher. When he was dominie at Cairnbanno he was recognised as a poet of some note. He was more enthusiastic about his verse than he was about his teaching, and this is what he had to say about the role of dominie:

A country dominie at best
Has little fog about his nest,
The chiel wha kens nae lack o' clink
Can just sough on, an' seenil think.*

Half a century later another Buchan poet, J. C. Milne, himself a headmaster, was asking 'Wha wid be a dominie?' Nobody with a grain of gumption, said Milne, would even think of it. But being a teacher and ultimately a dominie provided Ingram with an escape route from the poverty and squalor of the early weavers' towns. He wrote about life in those desperate days, about the norlan' climes and winter, 'the gruesome carl', battering the 'aul' clay biggins'. Some of his poems were rejected because it was said that 'hell was not delicately enough introduced'.

The Waggle is about the only thing in Cuminestown that hasn't changed since Ingram wrote about his boyhood there. From the hill you look west to the lovely Water of Idoch, which the Cuminestown painter James Cowie used as a background to many of his works. There is said to be a cairn on top of the hill called the Waggle Cairn, but I searched high and low for it and never found it. When I asked a farmer on the Waggle where it was he said he had never seen it — 'an' I've been here a' my life'.

The village itself is like most other Buchan communities of its size, quiet, unhurried, a little drawn into itself, almost hiding away from the outside world. I hoped I would come across some ancient inn where the Laird of Auchry had treated his compliant tenants to a dram and damned his drones for

*Fog — money. Seenil — seldom.

81

their laziness, but I never found it, although there are two hotels in the village.

The Peterhead-Banff turnpike, which cuts across central Buchan, was said by an old song to twist and twine around the knowes and hollows so much that you 'scarce could tell its ups fae doon'. Half a mile south of it is the farm of Cowbog, whose names comes from the Scots word *quaw*, meaning a kind of bog, a quagmire. It is here that the North Ugie Water has its source, 'taking its rise', as Dr John Pratt said, 'among moors and mosses and creeping through bogs and swamps', and it was on the fringes of this vast peatland that Buchan's four principal 'new towns' grew and flourished. Three of them were products of the 18th century — Cuminestown, the first, in 1763; New Byth, founded by James Urquhart of Byth in 1764; and New Pitsligo in 1787. New Deer, dragging its feet into the 19th century, followed in 1803.

Dr Pratt upset New Byth folk by saying that their village was 'in the vicinity of a bleak moss-bog'. He may have been tactless, but he was accurate enough. Both Cuminestown and New Byth were sited on high ridges of land on a watershed formed by the east-flowing headwaters of the North Ugie and streams going west to join the Deveron on the Aberdeenshire-Banffshire border.

New Byth's lofty situation is best seen when you approach it from the south, dipping down to the Burn of Monquhitter before struggling up a very steep brae into the village. The red sandstone of some of its houses lend character to little New Byth, but its charm is sadly marred by the harling that has taken place. 'It must have been a bonny village before that happened', I remarked to a local householder. She agreed, but said that the harling on her house had been done because the walls of the houses had been 'picket'. In other words, the weather had eaten into them.

The ghost of Ebenezer Gibb was on my tail when I walked through the village. Born in 1799, he was a shoemaker in New Byth for a large part of the 19th century, the period when it was famous for its souters. I have never been able to find out if it was quality or quantity that put it ahead of other soutering towns. There are no shoemakers there now, but when I mentioned this to one resident he commented, 'There's nae souters in places a lot bigger than this'. He was right, yet Buchan had more than its share of souters in the old days, their presence trumpeted by end-of-road signs like Souterford, Souterhill and Soutertown. I had two uncles who were souters, one in Lonmay, the other in Mintlaw.

Despite that, souters had always seemed to me to be gloomy people who worked in gloomy shops, surrounded by old boots, smelling of leather and spitting tackets from their teeth. I once saw a picture by Aberdeen's pioneering photographer, George Washington Wilson, of a village shoemaker in the 1880s. There he was, a little old man with a splayed white beard and a funny hat, wearing crumpled trousers and a jacket with sleeves turned up, a leather apron dropping down from under his beard to his lap. He wore a pair of plain spectacles on his nose and was busy stitching a pair of ploughman's tackety boots.

This gnome-like figure, who bore little resemblance to my shoemaking relatives, looked like the Rumpelstiltskin of the soutering world. He might have been a character from the Buchan comic song, 'The Souters' Feast', which Gavin Greig said was 'about as humorous a folk-song as we have ever come across'.

Greig thought it originated in central Buchan, possibly Maud. It is a 'nonsense' song about a celebration that took place when a souter's wife gave birth to a son. Souters came to it from Aberdeen and 'hine frae Perth', from Turra, Elgin and Aberdour, 'drivin' in a coach-and-four'. Some came in from Peterhead, 'wi' fient a teeth in a' their heid', having lost them chewing the leather to soften it. Not all were welcome:

An ill-faured skyple cam' frae Crimon',
A perfect scunner to the women,
A muckle hypal haveless loon
Frae the Fite Steen cam' hoiterin' doon.

For all the fame of its cobblers, New Byth didn't get a mention in 'The Souters' Feast', or not, at any rate, in the version published by Greig in his *Folk-Song of the North-East*. Greig said there was another version of the song, but he gave only the first verse, which was about a souter who came from Oyne (or Een, as the locals pronounce it) 'ridin' on a muckle preen'. He declined to give the rest of it because 'it would not make for edification'.

Maybe it was the smell of boot-leather that tickled people's nostrils when they arrived in New Byth a century ago, but today a more potent smell reminds you that this is the Land of Peat as well as the Land of Plenty. Going east to New Pitsligo, the peat mosses hem you in on either side, and when you enter the village the pungent smell of peat reek makes you sniff the air like the original Bisto kid. James Milne, writing about New Pitsligo last century, said that peat smoke hung like a cloud over the village. 'It permeated every nook and cranny of the houses, and the villagers carried it about with them in their reek-drenched clothing'.

I saw the Pitsligo mosses when I stayed with relatives in Buchan as a youngster, but I had no idea how big a role they played in the lives of the men and women who built New Pitsligo. Every feuar had his own section of moss free and some hired 'mossers' to cut the peat for them. If the weather was good these experts with the flauchter spades never left the moss from Monday morning to Saturday night, sleeping in rough shacks and having their food carried in to them. They could make up to £3 a week, which was a good wage in those days. Settlers were attracted to the village by the 'inexhaustible quantity of moss', along with fine water, an abundance of stone for building — and the fact that there was a Stampmaster living near the village. There was also a runner who carried letters to and from the Post Office at Strichen.

The man who built New Pitsligo also built Edinburgh's New Town. He was Sir William Forbes, banker, author and friend of Sir Walter Scott, and he was probably less interested in financial gain than in perpetuating the old name of

Pitsligo. His grandmother was a sister of the fourth and last Lord Pitsligo, whose escape after the '45 Rising became part of Buchan's lore. Sir William built the Pitsligo Arms Hotel, which was 'fitted up in sufficient style and comfort as to be made the headquarters of the family when in the neighbourhood'. The hotel is still there today.

While Sir William sat in the Pitsligo Arms watching the village grow, the cottars who were creating his new Jerusalem had to put up with a good deal less style and comfort. Their buts-and-bens were cramped and uncomfortable, some with garrets which took a few beds. There wasn't one bathroom in the village; washing was done in a wooden bath tub.

With New Pitsligo built on the slopes of Turlundie Hill, the village has a High Street and a Low Street running parallel to each other. Drainage originally took the form of open stone gutters, which meant that people on one side of the High Street, where the houses were built at a lower level than the road, had to put up with the stench of sewage a couple of yards from their front doors. These gutters are still there, with 'bridges' built across them from the street to the doors.

The village was built on the site of a farm called Cavoch, pronounced Kyaak, although old records show it as Old Cavoch, Old Keak, New Cake and Old Cake. Presumably New Cake was Sir William Forbes's 'new town'. Settlers taking a bite of it must have found it little to their taste, for it was anything but promising — it amounted to 'patches of miserably cultivated fields scattered here and there on the moor and moss'. But the founder laid out miles of roads and planted thousands of trees and by 1864 the place had grown to become the largest village in Scotland, with a population of 2000 people.

New Deer was more familiar to me than New Pitsligo in my boyhood, for it was only two miles from Shevado, where my uncle was grieve on the Brucklay estate. In later years, I was drawn to it by the wondrous names that I saw on maps of Buchan ... Hardbedlam, Fadliedyke, Pitfoskie, Frostiebrae, and Pundlercroft, which was once the home of a *pundler*, an impounder of stray animals. Place-names are signposts to the past. They tell you about people and places, about fairy-tale castles and forgotten battles; Brucehill, for instance, where Edward, brother of Robert the Bruce, spent the night before defeating the Comyn's at Aikey Brae, and Bennygoak, which the poet Flora Garry called the Hill of the Cuckoo — 'the bird 'at gid this hull its name, Yon bird ye niver see'.

Auchmaliddie, south of New Deer, was where there were cockerty steens, rocking stones, including the Muckle Stane of Auchmaliddie. The Muckle Stane had stopped rocking when Dr Pratt saw it; it was 'a mere mass of rock'. The Ordnance Survey map shows standing stones on the site of the Muckle Stane, and there were also standing stones on the Hill of Culsh.

The hill is crowned by a steeple-like tower built in 1875 by the tenants of Brucklay estate in memory of William Dingwall-Fordyce, M.P. There is a spiral staircase in the tower and from the higher level a breathtaking view of the Buchan landscape unfolds, stretching away to where the flares of the St Fergus gas terminal flicker over the coast. I counted off the landmarks which Pratt's *Buchan* said could be seen from the monument . . . the spires of Peterhead to the east, Bennachie to the west, the Foudland hills, the hills at Banff and Cullen, and away to the north the misty outline of Ben Rinnes in Moray.

Then I was drawn to more familiar countryside. Below me, less than two miles away, were the woods of Brucklay. Just noticeable among the trees were the ruins of Brucklay Castle, the 'old castlellated Mansion' which Dr Pratt said combined 'the grandeur of the middle ages with the elegance of the present'.

Away on my left, in a field bordering Brucklay, was another ruined castle, Fedderate. Fedderate, which is thought to date from the early 13th century, had none of the grandeur of Brucklay. It was built for battle, not beauty, and Buchan's squelching bogs provided the proper setting for it. It was surrounded 'partly by a fosse (moat) and partly by a morass', so that the approach to it was by a causeway and a drawbridge. They say that the Culsh standing stones were removed to build a manse, but Fedderate's stones were taken away by hard-headed farmers to build dykes and barns.

The mighty fortalice has been reduced to two sinister-looking granite towers. Standing under them, I couldn't help thinking of Mains Crawford, whose ghost must have been lurking about Brucklay when I was a boy at Shevado. The Crawfords had some connection with the castle and Mains Crawford, a man of great strength, is said to have lost his eyesight in a contest with the Devil to see who could lift a huge boulder known as Mains Crawford's stone. No stone lies at Fedderate now, so perhaps the De'il won.

It was at the Hill of Culsh that I took my leave of New Deer, remembering that many people who had fostered Buchan's cultural heritage had been buried in the kirkyard next to the Dingwall-Fordyce monument. Gavin Greig, the folk-song collector, had been laid to rest there, as had Bertie Forbes, the Whitehill lad who, encouraged by Greig, had gone to America and founded the 'Forbes Magazine'. His body was returned from New York and interred at Culsh.

Near the entrance to the cemetery I passed a gravestone which had the name of James Fowlie Dickie on it, while under it were the words, 'One of Nature's gentlemen'. The tribute was paid to Dickie, the great Buchan fiddler, by James Scott Skinner, the Strathspey King. Seven or eight years ago I was taken on a tour of this part of Buchan by Jim Duncan, who was so much behind the setting up of the Buchan Heritage Society. Jim was married to Ivory, Dickie's daughter, and I remember him telling me that concern for the Buchan language should not be confined to the Doric. There was, he said, also the language of music — Buchan fiddle music.

CHAPTER TEN

The Road to Meiklebogs

There's a road to heaven and a road to hell, but damn the road to Meiklebogs . . .

When Lewis Grassic Gibbon wrote that line he was conjuring up a picture of a farm in the Mearns, Dalziel's farm, whose master 'looked like a Highland bull, with his hair and his horns and maybe other things', but it was to the Howe of Auchterless, on the western fringes of Buchan, that I went in search of the *real* Meiklebogs, chasing those half-forgotten lines from *Cloud Howe*.

If you look at a map of the area you will find the authentic Meiklebogs hiding away in the Howe not far from Hillhead of Seggat, where Gibbon was born. Gibbon dipped into his own background for a number of places in his *Scots Quair*. One was Segget, a name he plucked from his memories of Buchan and, with the change of one letter, gave to the spinners' town in the Mearns where 'a tink-like lot of creatures' danced and fought and raised hell's delight. The other was Meiklebogs.

When I took the road to Meiklebogs it was to find out how it compared with Gibbon's imaginary farm toun, but I was also searching for a sense of the past, for some tangible reminder of what life was like in the land where Gibbon spent his childhood. I was breathing in the smells that touched his nostrils long after he had broken away from his roots . . . 'the smells of the earth and clover, the smell of sheep in winter buchts, the keen metallic smell of new-ploughed earth, the biting smells of whin-burning'.

First, however, I went to Seggat — to 'Hillies' — and found myself chasing ghosts. I had been there eight years before and had found it ruinous and neglected, 'like all the other old farm touns that were once scattered across the face of Buchan'. It was a depressing sight, but I thought that things might have changed.

I went down an overgrown farm track, rutted and 'sossed' like the road to Meiklebogs, and at the end of it the cottar house I was looking for was even more derelict, the wind keening through broken windows, banging half-broken doors and rattling bits of discarded machinery as if in protest at what had happened to 'Hillies'. It was cold and dreich. The rain spattered off worn slates, mirroring the 'grey, grey' life that Gibbon wrote about — the rain and sleet . . . the wind blowing on 'ungarmented floors' . . . 'ploughmen in sodden bothies on the farms outbye'.

Here, there was nothing but emptiness and desolation. Far away in the Mearns, where Gibbon's novels had scandalised local folk and made him 'the speak o' the place', they had opened a visitors' centre in his memory, although some people with long memories refused to give a penny to it. 'He just blackened folk here', they said. There are some people in the Howe who feel aggrieved about all this fuss in the Mearns, while up in Buchan, where James Leslie Mitchell spent the first seven years of his life, there is nothing to show that he ever existed.

Hillhead of Seggat is on land farmed by George Chalmers, Midhill of Seggat, whose wife has for long been concerned that Buchan's links with the author of *Sunset Song* have been ignored. She makes the point that this is Lewis Grassic Gibbon's *birthplace*, not the Mearns. One of the problems is that estate owners are reluctant to plough money into derelict farms, which is why 'Hillies' had deteriorated since the last time I saw it. Before George came to Seggat (his son works the neighbouring farm of Gordontown of Seggat) the gable-end of the house had been taken out and a huge barn door put in its place. Now the front parlour of 'Hillies', where Gibbon played as a boy, houses a combine-harvester.

The byre had been brought back into use. Cattle shouldered each out of the way to get a look at the stranger who had come to 'Hillies'. The midden next to the byre was empty, wet with slush from intermittent showers of sleet and snow. The yard was a porridge-like mess of mud and water. I looked at the upstairs room, where the thin, bare branches of a tree were tap-tapping on broken window-panes, and thought of the youngster who had once looked down on such a scene, seeing 'brown beasts oozing through the midden glaur'.

In *The Thirteenth Disciple*, which he wrote as J. Leslie Mitchell, young Malcolm Maudslay had been reading 'those Catholic writers who, for some obscure reason, champion the peasant and his state as the ideal state'. He was 'unprintably sceptical as to Mr Chesterton or his chelas ever having grubbed a livelihood from hungry acres of red clay', and he visualised him 'sentenced to pass three years at Chapel o' Seddel as hired man . . . staggering across the slimy floors of Chapel o' Seddel byre behind a barrow-load of reeking manure'.

The reference to 'hungry acres of red clay' seemed to place the Chapel o' Seddel in the Mearns, but here again there is an interplay of fact and fiction. The Chapel o' Seddel is clearly the Chapel of Seggat, which is half a mile from Hillhead. There was a kirkton at Seggat at one time, but only a fragment of the chapel remains and the name now belongs to a large farm. *The Thirteenth Disciple*, published in 1931, was Mitchell's second novel. There is little doubt that it was an autobiographical novel and it has been said that it drew on his early days in the Mearns, but I believe that 'Hillies' and the Howe of Auchterless have a stronger claim.

Before I left Hillhead I looked for signs of a chaumer or a bothy, for it was in these uninviting quarters, with their wooden beds, their kists and cooking pots, that you felt the heartbeat of Buchan. But there was no bothy at 'Hillies', and I found the explanation of why this was so in another passage in *The Thirteenth Disciple*, in which Mitchell, describing the Chapel o' Seddel farm, said that John Maudslay kept one hired man, who 'slept in a garret under the eaves'. So I left 'Hillies' and took the road to Meiklebogs, and as I drove through the Howe of Auchterless I had one eye on the road and one eye open for those 'sodden bothies on the farms outbye'.

The farm of Meiklebogs lies to the south of Auchterless. The farmer, Herbert Singer, was out when I arrived, but Joyce, his wife, presented me with a problem when I said I was looking for the Meiklebogs of *Cloud Howe*. She told me that there were three Meiklebogs in *this* Howe. One was the Singer's place, the second was Alex Sim's farm just up the road, and the third — here she pointed to a farm across the fields — had changed its name to the Bogs of Rothie. As if that wasn't enough, there had been a fourth Meiklebogs — Meiklebogs Croft — until it was taken over by the larger farm.

It wasn't until Mrs Singer saw a TV production of *Sunset Song* that she learned about the Meiklebogs in Gibbon's novel. She realised that it wasn't *her* Meiklebogs on the screen, but she wondered if Grassic Gibbon had known about the farm and 'borrowed' its name. She wasn't sure, and still isn't sure, but I had the feeling that she would like to think that the Singer farm was immortalised on the 'telly'. It probably had a greater claim than the other Meiklebogs, for it was the oldest, although at 70 acres it was also the smallest.

The farm, which had been worked by Bert Singer's father and grandfather, was owned by the Rothie estate. The lands of Rothie had originally been the property of two feudal owners, Norman and Brisbane, and from this came Rothienorman, the district and the village, and Rothiebrisbane, a farm near Meiklebogs. In 1928 the Singers bought the farm, and old deeds show that in addition to a cash payment they had to stump up another 'payment' of six hens.

From Meiklebogs I set off to find the farm of Brownhill at Auchterless, which I had been told still had a furnished bothy with wooden bunks and chaff-filled mattresses, but the confusion of Meiklebogs paled into insignificance alongside the muddle of Brownhills. There seemed to be Brownhills all over Buchan. I have sometimes wondered about the origin of the name, supposing it to have something to do with the colour of the earth. On the other hand, some place-name experts trace it back to the old Scots word *brownie*, meaning 'a kind of fairy'. A brownie was supposed to be a benevolent sprite that haunted old farmhouses and did 'many useful services overnight to the family'.

There is a Brown Hill less than a mile from Meiklebogs, and a Brownhill Farm down a narrow road to the south of it. But it was no brosy Buchan farmer who answered my knock on the door; instead, a plump-faced American citizen whose business was saving souls, not sowing neeps, greeted me. He was a Baptist minister who had been preaching in Buchan for the past nine years and, despite the flurries of snow blowing across his yard, clearly thought that *this* was God's country. I went on my way, hoping that a friendly brownie would point me in the right direction.

The Brownhill I was looking for turned out to be a road-side farm some five miles south of Turriff. I had read about it in *Wirds an' Wark 'e Seasons Roon*, a superb study of life on an Aberdeenshire farm by Alexander Fenton. Sandy Fenton is an internationally recognised authority on Scottish rural life and in 1951 was appointed to the newly-created Chair of Scottish Ethnology at Edinburgh University. He is himself an Auchterless loon and the material for *Wirds an' Wark* came from many years of talking and working with the late James Hunter of Brownhill.

The farmer's son, Jim Hunter, is still at Brownhill, although the scenes that Professor Fenton wrote about — shimmin' neeps and dragging coles with a horse-drawn hay-gatherer called a tummlin-tam — have long since gone. The fields are let out now and life slips past Brownhill as traffic roars up the road to Turra. Jim's sister, Evelyn, is married to Sandy Fenton, and to my surprise it was Mrs Fenton who answered my knock on the door. She frequently comes up from Edinburgh to stay with her brother.

She was born at Brownhill. We chatted about the old days and about chaumers and bothies. There has always been some confusion about the two types of accommodation. Evelyn Fenton said that bothies were more prevalent farther south, while in the North-east the single men slept in chaumers. In *Wirds an' Wark*, Sandy Fenton said there was no bothying in this area and the fee'd men got their meals in the farm kitchen.

Jim Hunter said that the Brownhill bailie (cattleman), Willie Beddie (they pronounced it Beedie) got his food in the house. There was only one wooden bed in the Brownhill chaumer and it was occupied by Willie, who had the luxury of a chaff mattress. Willie worked for the Hunters for over thirty years and Evelyn Fenton said that a lot of space in his chaumer was taken up by his two kists, otherwise there would have been room for another bed. Now there weren't any beds, or kists for that matter, for Jim used it as a store.

Jim took me round to have a look at the chaumer. There was a melancholy air about the farm, a feeling that life had oozed out of it. The neep shed and the hay-loft above it were deserted, and to the right of the chaumer was the gig-shed. Jim opened the chaumer door and I found my entry blocked by boxes that he had stored away there. Mrs Fenton had said that she would be ashamed to show me the chaumer, the state it was in. Still, poking my head round the door, seeing the pine walls and the fire against the gable, I was able to imagine how it must have been when Brownhill was in its hey-day.

When I left Brownhill I was heading for another farm and another chaumer I had known when my brothers and I hyowed neeps as lads at Aul' Jimmy Cummine's farm, Cauldwells, near New Byth. He was my uncle, but it was left to his son, Jimmy, to run the farm, and, disapproving of toon loons wasting their time on holidays, he armed us with hoes and sent us out to the turnip fields to help with the singling. It did little for the productivity of Cauldwells, but it taught us a lot about a back-breaking job universally hated by farm workers. We were young to be 'orra loons', but Jimmy Cummine may have thought that our youth was no disadvantage and that our size was an asset. William Alexander, in *Northern Rural Life*, told how the Laird of Inveramsay used hoes with shafts only two and a half feet long. He thought that the nearer the men were to work the better the job they would make.

So from Brownhill I went north by the Howe of Teuchar to Cuminestown and on by Auchry to Cauldwells to find out what had happened to my Cummine relatives. After all these years there was never any danger that I would miss it, for at the road end I came upon a big sign announcing, 'Cauldwells D. A. Taylor'. The track to the farm did a sharp, dog-leg turn to the left and I could see someone walking down towards the farm-house. Then a boy on a bike came pedalling up towards him, and suddenly I saw a mirror image of myself wandering up that dusty farm track in the years before the war. As I went down to the farm it looked as if nothing had changed, but I was wrong about that.

The two people I had seen were waiting at the farmhouse to have a look at the stranger. One was the farmer, Andy Taylor, the other his grandson, nine-year-old Mark. A minute later we were joined by Mark's father, David — the D. A. Taylor of the road sign — who now lives at Cauldwells; Andy has a house not far from the farm. To my surprise I was told that Andy not only knew the Cummines but had taken over the farm from my cousin. When we were chatting about Aul' Jimmy Cummine the conversation seemed to be at cross-purposes. It suddenly struck me that while I was talking about Aul' Jimmy, my uncle, the Aul' Jimmy they were talking about was my cousin. The Taylors knew 'young' Jim only as an old man, and they had never known my uncle at all. I learned, too, that all the Cummines of Cauldwells were dead ... Uncle Jimmy, my Aunt Aggie, cousin John, who had been a vet in Strichen, cousin Joe, an engineer in Inverurie, Carrie, who had been a teacher, and Jimmy, the oldest, who had become the farmer at Cauldwells. Jimmy was the last to go.

Andy Taylor originally worked the neighbouring croft of East Millseat, but when it was taken into another, larger farm he moved to Cauldwells. That was in 1967, and since then Cauldwells had itself absorbed three small crofts. In my uncle's day it had run to 120 acres, but it had doubled in size and was now 260 acres. They showed me round the farm, pointing out the new buildings that had gone up, one using the old steading wall but demolishing the rest of it. The farm-house had also changed, or at least the back of it, where they were building an extension. The front was exactly the same as it always had been, probably since the end of last century. David pointed out a stone on the gable where you could just make out the date 1886.

Whatever else I had forgotten over the years, three things at Cauldwells had remained in my mind — the memory of hyowin' neeps, of puddling at the farm dam, and of prowling about the chaumer. We sailed 'boaties' on the dam and watched the ducks splashing in the water. I still have a faded snapshot of myself sitting on the back of a Clydesdale at the edge of the dam, with the farmhouse in the background.

The dam had been at the front of the house, but the Taylors had dried it up and turned it into a lawn.

'I wish you'd kept it', I said.

I wasn't the only one who thought that. My cousin Carrie had come back to Cauldwells a few years before and had said the same thing.

Water from the dam had worked a threshing mill, whose crumbling walls could be seen a short distance from the farm-house. The water had come from a source near the farm of Rush, which I could see on the other side of the Cumines-town road. From there a pipe wriggled its way under the fields to the Cauldwell dam. 'Rush' and 'Rashie' are names that can be seen in many parts of Buchan, soggy reminders of what lies under your feet. Andy and David Taylor agreed that this was land that was 'wet, wet, wet'.

So that was the dam. When I arrived at the farm I looked for the chaumer and could see no sign of it, but a clue to its whereabouts lay in the shapes of doors and windows along the wall of the old steading, all filled in with stone. They were where the cart shed and stables had been, and between them was a small section showing the outlines of a door and a window. 'That was the chaumer', said Andy. The past had been sealed off to make way for a modern farm building. The shapes on the wall were symbols of the old farming ways in Buchan . . . of cairts and Clydesdales, brose caups and nicky-tams, and maybe the scrape of a fiddle and the sound of an old bothy ballad.

To a lad from the town the word 'chaumer' was foreign-sounding, and, in fact, it was said to come from the French *chaumiere*, which meant a chamber. Somehow or other, *chaumieres* sat uneasily with nicky-tams and tackety boots. A chamber was for the laird in his fancy mansion.

There were rumours and gossip about the scandalous things that went on in chaumers, but I knew nothing of that when I was singling neeps on my uncle's farm. The only introduction I got to sex at Cauldwells was when I was allowed to watch a bull earning its keep. But, in fact, chaumers were condemned by ministers as 'hot-beds of immorality and vice'.

Hot-blooded farm workers suffered from what one writer called 'priapic intent', which meant that they lusted after the kitchie deems. The snapshot showing me astride a Clydesdale at the Cauldwells dam has a young girl holding the horse's head, but I have no recollection of her. I have sometimes wondered if she was the farm's kitchie deem, and if any red-blooded baillie had knocked on the window of her bedroom at night, which often happened. A kitchie deem's room was usually tiny and sparsely furnished — 'a hole into which she could creep at night'. As John R. Allan wrote, 'There the domestics spent their dreary nights diversified by spasms of bucolic love'.

A ballad called 'Auld Luckie of Brunties' told how the farmer's wife kept an eye open for 'rovin' young men'. Anyone found with a servant was fined:

Auld Luckie she's a wily ane,
And she does watch the toon,
And ilka lad that she does catch
She fines him half-a-crown.

Sweeping the chaumer and making the men's beds were part of the kitchie deem's duties, and, not surprisingly, one thing led to another:

Jean McPherson makes my bed
She sleeps between me and the wa',
And when I climb in ower at nicht
She says, 'Buchan Geordie, ca' awa'.

All these ongoings made me wonder if there had been any Buchan Geordies at Cauldwells. The Taylors told me that the farm had been a three-horse place, although one was an old beast used for carrying cart-loads of neeps and doing other odd jobs — an 'orra horse', like an orra man. There had been a horseman, a bailie and an orra loon. So there would probably have been three men in the chaumer, although Andy remembered hearing that one had lived in an old house up the road and not in the chaumer.

When I left Cauldwells and its blocked-up chaumer I went south to the village of Garmond, which was established shortly after Cuminestown came into being. Only a mile separates the villages. Why the Cumines felt it necessary to create two weaving communities so close to each other is a mystery. The locals always speak of it as The Garmond. Coming to it from Cauldwells you find yourself on a steep hill which drops down sharply to the Burn of Monquhitter. The houses are spaced out on this brae in an almost haphazard fashion. In 1871 there were 268 people living there, 300 *more* than in Cuminestown, but Garmond has become the Cinderella of the two.

I went to Garmond for two reasons — or, rather, for two people. For a start, I had been told by Andy Taylor that Jimmy Cummine and his wife, Margaret, had moved to the village when he retired. Margaret, who had been a teacher, still lived there in a house almost at the bottom of the brae. I had heard of her, but we had never met, and when we did we exchanged notes about the Cummines and Cauldwells. I spoke about hyowin' neeps on the farm as a boy. 'Aye', she said. 'Nobody went there for a holiday. They all had to work'.

The other person who drew me to The Garmond was a legendary figure called Francie Jamieson, better known as Fruncie Markis. He got his nickname through his father, William Jamieson, a handsome, gentlemanly fellow who rode into Garmond one day to visit his married sister and made a hit with the weaving ladies. His image was enhanced by his sister's description of him as 'a braw and pretty man'. She said he had 'nae a marra (equal) in a' the north ither than the Marquis o' Huntly'. From then on William was known as 'Marquis', a name that Francie duly inherited.

When I was at Cauldwells I asked Andy Taylor about Fruncie. He knew of him, for Fruncie had come from the Crudie area, not much more than a mile north of Cauldwells. He told me one of the classic tales about Fruncie Markis — about how he once tried to race a train down the Buchan line. I was to hear many different versions of the same story as I followed Fruncie through the braes and bogs of Buchan. Andy knew where the ruins of Fruncie's cottar house could be found in the Crudie area, near the Granite Croft. That was where I was heading when I went down the hill from Margaret Cummine's house and took my farewell of The Garmond.

CHAPTER ELEVEN

Francie's Oxter Pipes

Up on the braes of Clochforbie the skies seem vast, the vistas endless. The folk who live there are liable to throw back in your teeth the slur that apart from Mormond there isn't a hill in Buchan worth mentioning. They will count them out for you . . . the Hill of Cook, Overbrae, Bracklamore, the Hill of Fishrie. When Dr Pratt wrote dismissively about New Byth and its peat bog, the Rev. Thomas M'William, minister of New Byth and author of *A Quiet Buchan Parish*, said that supercilious people like him should go to the Hill of Fishrie and look around them.

He reeled off the names of hills you could see from Fishrie — Ben Rinnes, the Tap o' Noth, the Bin of Cullen, Bennachie, Knock, the Hill of Durn . . . on and on he went, pouring out a litany of hilltops and ending up with what was to him the most exhilarating sight of all — 'the smoke of a train between Portsoy and Tillynaught'. He called this the Pride of the Railway and wondered if it might ever come nearer to New Byth. It never did. Now the railway has gone and there is no smoke, no train, and precious little pride.

'Perhaps you may need old Francie Jamieson's telescope', he said, 'but he will be quite willing to let you look through it'.

It was the sound of Francie's oxter pipes, not the prospect of looking through his telescope, that lured me into these hills. He had become a kind of Pied Piper to me. I followed him into the gently undulating braes of Byth and up by the peat bogs of Bracklamore, searching for the little thackit hoosie where he lived, looking for anyone who could tell me about one of the great Buchan characters of last century. He had been dead for nearly a hundred years, yet they still talked

99

about him. He rarely got his 'Sunday name'. He was born Francis, but he was always known as Fruncie, or, to give him his full name, Fruncie *Markis*. The Markis or Marquis was added because he looked like the Marquis of Huntly.

When they were building the turnpike from Peterhead to Banff the funds ran out and the road suddenly came to an abrupt end at Auchnagorth, two miles north of New Byth, on the edge of a seemingly endless expanse of moorland. It became temporarily a road to nowhere, so that superstitious people looked upon the little-known area beyond it as 'an eerie, uncanny place'. It may not be that today, but the great peatlands that spread around the Hills of Fishrie and Overbrae give it a feeling of intense isolation.

That was another reason why I had come to this part of the North-east. It was different from the rest of Buchan. Down on the old turnpike, now a fast road from Fraserburgh to Banff, the traffic goes roaring past with blinkered eyes, past the Woods of Byth and the Hill of Cook, past little Crudie and the road to Shalloch, sweeping on to Macduff and the Deveron. But turn up one of those narrow side-roads and you are in another world, peppered with crofts and the ruins of crofts, with rutted, muddy farm tracks and 'roch' cluttered farmyards.

Up there it seems as if time stands still, as if nothing has changed since the Earl of Fife built 'a mud-and-thatch school' at Crudie a century and a half ago, put in a headmistress called Margaret Law, and told her to 'be kind to my little lairds'. The old clay biggin' was soon replaced by a stone building. Under Margaret Law it took in boarders and became so popular that 120 pupils were crowded into one room, while the boarders slept in the passage.

Margaret Law was the daughter of a Sutherland crofter evicted in the early 19th century Highland Clearances. In a remarkably generous gesture, the Earl of Fife gave over land to the evicted crofters so that they could be resettled. About 100 crofts appeared on the braes of Clochforbie. The name Crofts of Clochforbie can still be seen on maps, although most of them have vanished. Bill Irvine, who farms Nether Clochforbie, told me that there were five small crofts on Upper Clochforbie, but they eventually went 'back to the heather'. Now and then slates and tiles turn up when fields are being ploughed.

So this was Francis Jamieson's homeland, a sprawling, windswept corner of Buchan where change comes slowly, but is nevertheless taking place, where new houses are going up and new faces are being seen, and where the sound of a Sassenach tongue no longer brings a quizzical look and a lift of the eyebrow. Francie would probably have had a few harsh things to say about it; he was like Jamie Fleeman, nobody's fool, never a man to mince his words.

He was a unique and colourful character, not only an athlete but a talented musician — a master with the cello, an angel with the fiddle, and a devil with the oxter pipes. He was an admirer of the great Donald Dinnie and, while he may not have been able to match him on the field, he could run, jump, throw the hammer, putt the stone, sling the weight — and pull the sweirtree. This was a game in which two people sat on the ground holding a stick between them, each trying to pull the other up. More crudely, it was called the sweir-arse.

He had a gargantuan appetite and on one occasion, when he was invited to dine at Haddo House with his brother, a whole turkey was placed in front of him. Francie pulled off a leg, laid it on his brother's plate, and then proceeded to demolish the rest of the bird himself. There is another version of this story, telling how, when he went to an inn for his dinner, the servant girl laid the turkey on the table and went off to get a knife. When she came back she found him finishing off his meal.

'Ye didna tak' lang tae eat that!' she said.

'Na!' said Francie. 'It was a gey boss* bugger onywye'.

The tales about Francie are legion; some are apocryphal and time has muddied the facts about others. The turkey story,

*poor, hollow

101

for instance, was originally laid at the door of Joseph Sim, known as the Wonderful Boy of New Byth. Some reports say he was Francie's nephew, others are vague about their relationship. At any rate, Joseph, a talented fiddler, had a dance band and often teamed up with Francie to play at functions all over Buchan.

When I went in search of Francie's thackit hoosie I had little idea where to look. Nobody knew *exactly* where it was, so I chased my tail on a spider's web of narrow roads until I landed up on the Hill of Cook. Somebody said Francie had lived at No. 45, but No. 45 no longer existed. Then I remembered Andy Taylor, the farmer at Cauldwells, telling me to try the Granite Croft. Jim Allan, who has farmed there since 1945, came to the door. When I asked him where Francis Jamieson's croft had been he looked puzzled. 'Fruncie *Markis*', I prompted. The penny dropped. He waved his hand. 'Right here!' he said.

He took me to a small wood running from his farmyard to the road-end. The cottage had been on this site, but only the ruins of it remained when Jim saw it. There was a story that some of the trees had been cut down and the stumps used as tables and chairs, but Jim put paid to that yarn by telling me that *he* planted the wood a few years after moving into the Granite Croft. There was also a small garden near the farm road.

I have seen a photograph of Francie's cottar house, with Francie standing outside it wearing a tammy and white fustian trousers that made him the talk of New Byth. When he went to kirk he exchanged his tammy for a lum hat — the tallest lum hat in the district, it was said. In the picture he had his pipes under his oxter. One end of the house was his living quarters, while in the other end he kept his 'shelties' and a cow. Hens perched on the rafters. If you wanted to see all that is left of Fruncie Markis's thackit hoosie you would have to dig down under Jim Allan's steading. There was a big hole there at one time and he filled it in with the stones from the ruined house and made a foundation for the steading.

Jim also showed me a small redstone trough at the back of his house. It was, he said, either a hen's troch (trough) or a pig's troch and it came from the cottage. There were three 'trochs' at one time, but a chap who was interested in Francie turned up and took two of them away.

Jim had heard all the stories about Fruncie. It was said that he could get from his croft to New Byth in record time – he did it on stilts. This tall tale may have stemmed from the fact that he used oxter staffs after injuring his legs and was able to take 10ft. strides with them. He took big enough strides *without* oxter staffs when he attempted to race a train from Aikey Brae to Maud. He failed, and when the train puffed off into the distance he shook his fist and shouted after it the immortal words, 'Ye muckle black bugger! Gin I hid ye on the Moss o' Byth I'd hae gaen ye a reed face'.

It was said that the Jamieson family 'clowned its way through Buchan for half a century', and by all accounts that included Francie's sister, Jean Jamieson, who lived with him on the Hill of Cook. She was nicknamed the 'heel wadge', and Jim Allan told me how Francie had taken her to the New Byth Games to bring about a 'match' with the famous Donald Dinnie, who often competed there. The idea was that together they would produce a super-athlete, but Dinnie sensibly declined the offer. Jean also featured in another story about how the Jamiesons got their fuel by encouraging local lads to throw peats at them. When the peat carts passed their croft on the way back from the Mosses of Fishrie or Kinbeam, Jean cavorted about the field half-naked and, bending over, offered her rump as a target for the peat-throwers. They say that Fruncie and his sister always had a good stack of peats for the winter.

Francis Jamieson died on 19th September, 1903. The violin had been his favourite instrument and in his last years he would sit in his thackit hoosie and play some of the old tunes that he loved. He died in poverty; he no longer had his bass fiddle, his double-cased lever watch, or his telescope. He was buried in the New Cemetery at Byth.

When I left Jim Allan and the Granite Croft I headed north by the moors and peat mosses where Francie had earned his living 'takkin' in' bog and scrub, and draining and clearing forestland. I was searching for two other 'characters' who had lived out their lives in this remote North-east corner. Both were women — and both were to Buchan what Hannah Hauxwell was to the Yorkshire Dales. Hannah, if you remember, shot to fame twenty years ago when she became the subject of a TV documentary about her life on a desolate Yorkshire farm with no electricity and no running water. Several books were written about her.

Like Hannah Hauxwell, Babbie Stewart and Peggy Clark single-handedly worked their crofts on the braes of Monquhitter, scratching a meagre living from the reluctant soil, ploughing, planting, cutting peats from the mosses, caring for their 'beasties'. Like Hannah, they had no electricity or water. But they were never 'discovered' as Hannah had been; they had never been guests at a 'Woman of the Year' lunch in the Savoy Hotel in London, or taken to a garden party in Buckingham Palace. Yet their story was no less remarkable.

Babbie, who was 74, had been born and bred at Overbrae, not far from the hill from which, according to the Rev. Thomas McWilliam, you could see 'quite a wonderful distance' even without Francie's telescope. I asked Jim Allan how to get there, but his reply shocked me. Babbie was dead — buried only two weeks before my arrival. She had fallen ill with water retention in her legs and it had turned gangrenous. She had refused to leave her home.

'She was thrawn to the last', said Bill Irvine, who had done some of the heavy work on her 20-acre croft. 'It was just the kind of her. She thought she had to bide and look after her beasties'. She had three cows and 'six little beasties'. Bill thought her death was probably a blessing in disguise. 'If she had been half-roaded again', he said, 'she would have been back on that hill'.

I remembered Hannah Hauxwell's parting remark when

she had to give up her farm on the high Pennines. She loved the place and hated to leave it. 'In years to come', she said, 'if you see a ghost walking here you can be sure it will be me'. Maybe, I thought, as I drove up those narrow, twisting roads, Babbie's ghost will be doing the same.

Peggy Clark lived at the Shalloch, which lies east of Crudie, not far from the road to Banff. The name is of uncertain origin. One theory is that it comes from the Gaelic *seileach*, meaning willow, but there were no willows that I saw. 'Shaloch' is also an old Scots word meaning plentiful or abundant, which scarcely applied to Peggy's croft. I had been told by Jim Allan that she was not above using a few harsh words of her own when provoked — 'sweir words' he said — so I knocked timidly on her door and waited.

Peggy was a tiny woman, a 'wee wifukie', plump, rosy-cheeked, with a woollen toorie on her head, wellie boots on her feet, and thick woollen jerseys to keep out the Clochforbie cold. She was seventy-four years old. She *looked* like the crofterwoman she was, inured to her hard life, fiercely independent, turning a faintly disapproving eye on the changes that were taking place. She was in the middle of her 'denner', with a plate of fish and tatties in her hand, and I braced myself for a torrent of 'sweir words'. They never came, which may have been because Shep, her 7-year-old collie dog, took a liking to me. She invited me in.

Inside her 'but and ben', which had two rooms and an attic, it seemed as if the years had slipped away and left her stranded in a time-warp. This was the old Buchan, with the smell of peat reek in your nostrils, two big black pots on the fire, and a big black kettle hanging on the swey ... it reminded me of my grandfather's croft when I was a boy. Peggy told me that Babbie Stewart had had a 'rannie' in her lum. A rannie or rantle is a wooden or iron bar across the chimney, with a chain and pot-hook dropping down from it to the fire. This is known as the crook, and there is an old saying that something is 'as black's the crook'. Two wallie dogs eyed me from the mantelpiece, while above them were framed photographs blackened with peat smoke. 'The room gets fu' o' reek', said Peggy. 'The fire's afa reekie'.

There was a pail standing on a wooden chair. This was her water supply, for you didn't turn on the tap if you wanted water at the Shalloch – you simply dipped your cup in the pail. After years of carrying pails, water was brought to the croft from a neighbouring farm, and a pump installed outside Peggy's door, but she couldn't get used to it and went back to pails. The lighting came from paraffin lamps and a Tilly and if I had asked for the toilet I would have been directed to what looked like a large wooden box at the bottom of the garden – the 'ootside lavie'. I saw eggs in a glass-fronted cupboard and glanced anxiously at the ceiling, wondering if there were hens sitting in the rafters, as they had done in Francie Markis's hoosie, defecating into Francie's brose bowl.

Peggy sat at the table eating her fish and tatties, dropping fishy titbits to one of her three cats. The tablecloth was made up of old newspapers. She had looked after her parents for many years at their farm at Feithley of Inverkeithney, six or eight miles out of Turriff, and when her father died it was said that she would get the croft. It didn't work out that way and a place was found for her up in the Byth area. She had been at the Shalloch for over forty years. The old folk in the district had gone, she said, and the young ones had moved away to get jobs elsewhere.

She kept cattle. She had sold some beasts and got five weaned calves just before I was there. I asked her if she did heavy work on the croft. 'Na! Na!' she said. 'The tools are gaun aul', I'm gaun aul'.' Bill Irvine rents half of Peggy's grass – 'she didn't want ower mony beasties', he said. He also did jobs for her after she lost the services of a contractor. Hens and ducks scurried about the yard. 'If ye run een ower', she said, 'it'll cost ye £3'.

Life can be hard in the winter. Once she had been snowed up for nine weeks. Nothing on Sunday, she said, snow on Monday, and when she woke up on Tuesday it was level with the paling posts. Thirteen or fourteen of them got together, all friends, and they lasted out the storm. She came down one day to 'feed my beasties' and found that a stirk had choked on a neep. She got in touch with the vet, but he said he couldn't come because all the roads were blocked. No, they weren't, she told him, for they had been 'casting' the snow and it was clear enough to get through. So the vet came, put a choke rope down the stirk's throat, and that was that.

It turned out that she had known my cousin, John Cummine, from Cauldwells, who had been the vet at Strichen. He had been a good vet, but she had always dealt with the vets at Turra. Cauldwells is not much more than a couple of miles from the Shalloch and Peggy also knew John's brother, Jimmy, who had farmed there with my uncle, Aul' Jimmy, and had taken over after he died. Jimmy Cummine, in fact, had provided her with seed corn. It was a small world.

Peats glowed and sputtered on the black fire. 'It's afa reekie', she said again. People still cut peat on the old mosses, but they have to pay for it. It was £70 for a lair and you were allowed to take out 700 barrows. For smaller amounts the price was reduced. Peggy paid £55 for her lair and could take out 500 barrows, but she had to pay someone to cast the peat. The bigger problem was getting it transported to the Shalloch, where she spread the peats, set them up, dried and bagged them.

There had been a road to the Fishrie moss from her croft, but it had fallen into disuse and she had ploughed it up. The Moss of Fishrie was where I was going. We stood outside her door, looking down the garden to where a line of shorn trees marched along the dyke to the wooden 'bog'. Beyond it a tractor grumbled up the steep brae of a neighbouring field, cutting patterns on the peaty brown earth. The fields rolled away to a hazy horizon and Peggy pointed out the distant hills . . . Ben Rinnes, the Tap o' Noth with its 'cap' on, the Bin, and many more.

So I left my wee wifukie, who, despite what Jim Allan had said, had never uttered an ill word, but had been friendly and helpful. Before I left I asked her if she was happy and she said yes, and I steered my way out of her yard, watching out for the 'deuk' that would cost me £3, and headed back up the Shalloch road. Two miles on I turned off at Middlehill and bumped into the Moss of Fishrie.

The tarred road ended and I could see a wide stony track running through the moorland, with peat stacks spaced out in the heather. The moss grew and expanded, a dark brown never-never land relentlessly spreading away as far as the eye could see, devouring the countryside, reaching out to the crofts that trembled like doll's houses on the edge of it. The only relief from it was the track, pushing on through the moss and breaking off in different directions towards Bracklamore Hill. This is shown on old maps as 'empty land', and that's what it was, bereft of life.

From where I stood I calculated that it was two miles across that dreary landscape to the Den of Glasslaw. It was at a Lodge there that Peggy Clark paid her dues for the peat that came out of the Moss of Fishrie. Peggy of the reekie lums. I thought of an old rhyme I had heard:

Cyaard, Cyaak and Cairnywhing,
An' scum the lums o' Glassla.

Scum means to scrape clean, although why Glasslaw was singled out for lum-cleaning is anybody's guess. Cairnywhing is less than two miles to the south, Cyaak is how you pronounce Cavoch, the old name for New Pitsligo, and Cyaards were wool carders.

I left the 'empty land' and headed west towards the Banff road. I was looking for the Muckle or Grey Stane of Cloch-forbie, a noted landmark. I found it inside a field not very far from Bill Irvine's farm at Netherbrae. It was about 12ft. long, a recumbent stone, which is supposed to have a treasure buried beneath it. The story goes that when anyone tries to dig it up a voice from below is heard saying, 'Let it be!'

'Let it be! Let it be! . . .' Maybe the 'treasure' was the land itself, one of the last corners of Buchan to abandon the old ways and the old values. I went down the Clochforbie braes, reluctant to leave them, thinking of Francie Markis and his oxter pipes, and of the muckle black bugger of a train that defeated him. If only he had been able to run against it on the Moss o' Byth. Wouldn't that have been something?

CHAPTER TWELVE

The Laird of Delgatie

As I came in by Netherdale
At Turra market for tae fee,
I fell in wi' a farmer chiel
Fae the Barnyards o' Delgatie

The Barnyards of Delgatie can be seen, pristine white, on a brae above a back road running east from Turriff. It was there that a 'farmer chiel' told a horseman looking for a fee that if he worked for him he would get the best pair of horses he had ever set eyes on. They turned out to be 'naething but skin and bone'. The auld black horse sat on its rump and refused to move and the auld white mare was never able to get up at yokin time.

The 'Barnyards of Delgaty' was one of the most popular of the late 19th-century bothy ballads, sung by farm workers who knew only too well the tyranny of hard-hearted, tight-fisted 'farmer chiels'. There were other bothy ballads with the same message, but 'The Barnyards' was the best-known of the protest songs, its bitter words echoing down the years. As I made my way to Delgatie by the road from Turra I could almost hear that last despairing cry, 'Ye'll never catch me here again'.

The farm, which was one of six belonging to the Delgatie estate, overlooks the Woods of Delgatie. Through a long tunnel of trees a track opens out at the foot of Delgatie Castle, rising in brooding magnificence over a narrow loch which originally covered 12 acres of ground. It has now shrunk to half that size. There is nothing romantic about Delgatie, which is said to be one of the most ancient inhabited mansions in Buchan. It has never been prettied up for the public, with the result that it looks like a weary old warrior, bruised by the years, but it is none the worse for that.

This great six-storey castle, family home of the Hays of Erroll, carries the weight of history on its shoulders. Its origins go back to 1030, starting as a stone keep with a four-storey tower, but it was gradually added to and in 1570 was rebuilt. An oxen yoke hangs in the vestibule of the castle along with battle shields and other relics of the past and above the door of a nearby cottage is the Hay's coat-of-arms, incorporating two yokes, a reminder of the time when three farmers using yokes as weapons held a narrow pass against invading Danes in the Battle of Luncarty, near Perth. For this they were given the name of Haye (in Gaelic, *Garadh*, meaning a palisade or wall).

The castle passed out of the hands of the Hays when it was bought by the Duff family. Occupied by the army during the last war, it lay uninhabited for a number of years, but it was then given what amounted to a death sentence — architects declared it too far gone to save. Captain John Hay, returning from service in the Indian Army soon after the end of the war, had other ideas. He embarked on a mammoth task of restoration, fighting off ruin and decay in the same way that his forbears had fought off the Danes a thousand years ago. Instead of a yoke he used a mason's hammer.

The Laird of Delgatie is an accomplished mason. When he was in India his fellow-officers took their siesta after lunch and then played polo. Capt. Hay had no desire to rest or play polo; instead, he went off and joined the Sappers at their work so that he could learn the craft of masonry. The result was a life-long passion for the work. Today, tradesmen are seldom called in to do repairs at Delgatie — the Laird does them himself.

His mason's stamp is all over Delgatie ... in the bridges that cross the Delgatie Burn, in the fire tank which has a mill wheel set into a facade made from cobbles lifted in Aberdeen when the tramcars were swept away, and in the ponds and waterfall he was building when I was there.

'I'm the second best mason in Turriff', he said.

'Who's the best?' I asked.

'I leave them to argue that out', he replied.

The implication was that *he* was the best mason in Turriff, but he stopped short of saying so. It is a remark he often makes to inquisitive visitors. He is still as busy as he ever was, but now he has to sit down while carrying out his masonry work, something he probably regards as having a certain irony to it. There is a room in the castle called Mrs Hay's sitting room. Capt. Hay told everyone that he never had a sitting room because he never had time to sit down. Now into his nineties, he admits that his legs give him trouble and he has to sit down while working. His wife, Eve, died twenty years ago and he designed a tombstone to serve them both. It is in a kirkyard at Turriff.

The cottage on the approach to the castle, with its coat-of-arms and twin yokes, was originally a brewery. That was in the days when workers on the estate were given a gallon of ale every week. Today it is the home of Mrs Joan Johnson, who had a bakery and a delicatessen in Turriff before moving to Delgatie. She went there looking for a house — and ended up becoming estate factor. She is an indefatigable Jack — or Joan — of all trades, looking after the running of the estate, playing a leading role in opening up the castle to visitors, presiding over the tea room (her home made carrot cake is mouth-watering), and selling tickets at the castle entrance. Now and then the Laird will be in the vestibule taking in the money. It isn't often that you will find a Feudal Baron and Grandmaster of the Guild of Masons in Scotland handing out tickets to stately home visitors.

I wandered through the castle, climbing up a massive turn-pike stair that had a span of over 5ft. — the widest span of its kind in Scotland — going up and up until I had counted 97 steps and was 70ft. above the ground. In the Laird's private room an inscription over the fireplace read 'My Hoyp is in Ye Lord'.

Two of Delgatie's most important rooms are the Tulip Room and the Painted Room, dating back to the late 16th century. The walls of the Tulip Room were decorated with beautiful painted ladies holding tulips, but the Victorians painted them out. The reason, according to the information board written by Capt. Hay, was that the ladies were thought to be ill-clothed for the climate. I have a feeling that the Laird had his tongue in his cheek when he wrote that. Between the beams are old Scottish proverbs. Designs in gay colours are seen in the Painted Room, some showing strange animals with human heads. They are thought to be caricatures of people who lived in the castle at the time.

Two strange creatures of a different sort were on guard on either side of the doorway when I left the castle. They were unicorns, with metal fittings to hold the flags that fluttered from them when they were on the roof of the *Scotsman* building in Edinburgh. When plans were made to remove them from the *Scotsman* Capt. Hay made his way to the roof and asked the workmen if he could take them away. All right, they said, go ahead and take them — and, with knowing looks, held out their mason's tools to him.

The Captain took off his jacket, pulled down his tie, and got to work. When the astonished workmen saw that he knew what he was doing they pitched in and helped him. The unicorns were dismantled, taken down to ground level, and sent on their way to Delgatie.

No castle of any worth is complete without its ghost and Delgatie is no exception. Here, the ghost is a 6ft. tall, strong-minded 19-year-old 'meddlesome redhead' called Rohaise, who was mistress of the Laird of Delgatie when the castle was besieged by the forces of James VI in the 16th century. Rohaise (pronounced Rohaisha) gathered a few men together and held out under bombardment for six weeks until the west wall collapsed, by which time the defenders had escaped down passages leading to Craigston Castle and fled to France.

Now, Rohaise is said to visit any man who is sleeping alone in one of the rooms in the castle.

Hubert Fenwick, a well-known author and architectural historian, wrote about the Delgatie haunting in his book, *Scotland's Castles* in 1976. Fenwick, who was brought up at Cuminestown and knew the Turriff area as a boy, made no mention of Rohaise, simply referring to 'the ghost at Delgatie'. But he was closer to the Delgatie wraith than most people, for his father 'was Pisky rector and exorcised the ghost'. At that time the castle was owned by the Ainslie family and Mrs Ainslie, who was Russian and of the Orthodox faith, insisted on Fenwick's father 'coming along with bell, book and candle and getting rid of the ghost'.

Rachel Grant-Duff-Ainslie was said to be psychic and her dreams led to a number of disturbing discoveries in the castle. She dreamed that something would be found behind the wall of a turret room and when it was opened up the body of a crouching monk or nun was seen. It crumbled to dust as soon as the air touched it, leaving a shin bone chained to the wall. In another dream she saw a secret room which could be reached by climbing up the back of a huge open fireplace. When a footman was sent to investigate he found religious relics hidden in what was probably a priest's hiding place.

I left Delgatie, its Barnyards and its ghosts, thinking of the disillusioned farm chiel and his skin-and-bones horses. 'Ye'll never catch me here again', he cried. If he had still been around today he would have been sorely tempted by Joan Johnson's home-made carrot cake. Farther down the Deveron valley I was looking for another castle which I thought might boast a wraith or two. The Castle of King Edward (or Kin-Edar) was the seat of the Comyn Earls of Buchan until Bruce wasted it in the 'herschip' of Buchan in 1308. There could have been little left of the Comyn stronghold after Bruce's men had done their worst, but Charles Cordiner, an 18th century artist given to putting historical events into exaggerated settings, showed the castle, or the remains of a later castle built on its foundations, standing on a small hill near a bridge

over the Burn of Fisherie. It was a powerful, highly romanti-
cised painting in which one massive tower dominated the
heavily-wooded mound.

That was in 1782, but when Dr John Pratt turned up at
Kineddar a century later he found only 'a shapeless heap of
ruin'. Now, with yet another century gone, you would scarcely
know that anything at all had been mouldering away there all
these years. The farmer at Castletown showed me how to get
to what was left of the castle by a narrow footpath running
uphill from a bridge over the Turriff-Banff road.

The area is so heavily wooded that it is almost impenetrable.
Odd chunks of masonry could be seen among the nettles and
weeds as I climbed above the Fisherie burn. At the top of the
hill an ugly finger of stone rose through the undergrowth.
This was all that remained of the ruined tower in Cordiner's
painting . . . 'a forlorn remnant', as Dr Pratt put it, 'of a great-
ness which could measure itself even with royalty'. History
was buried in a tangle of weeds, yet it was here that Comyn
power crumbled and from here that Bruce's men were sent out
to 'burn all Buchan from end to end, sparing none'.

John Pratt mentioned two roads running from Turriff to
Banff, one passing King Edward Castle, the other following
the Deveron to the Castle of Eden. This ancient fortalice
stands at a road junction near the Deveron, where the river
makes a great bend on its final run to the sea. It was built by
the Meldrums, but passed to the Leslies and later to the
Duffs. The farmer was counting his sheep under its broken
walls when I passed, clearly unperturbed by the curse that lay
over it. They say that a servant upset the Laird of Eden and
was condemned to die. His wife pleaded with the laird to
spare her husband's life, but he ignored her. So she laid a
curse on him:

Caul micht the wind blaw
Aboot the yetts o' Eden.

Whatever the truth of the story, the caul North-east winds

must have blown mightily about the yetts of this 16th century stronghold, for like its big brother farther up the valley it is now a ruin, its east gable gone and the rest of it looking as if it might go the same way before long.

Beyond Eden Castle are the woods of Montcoffer and the Bridge of Alvah. Montcoffer House stands on a hill overlooking the rich farmlands of the Deveron valley. It was built in 1680 by Peter (Patrick) Russell and in 1755 William Duff of Braco bought it from Alexander Russell. The Russells and Duffs became involved in a series of lawsuits over fishing rights on the Deveron and in the end the Russells gave up Montcoffer in disgust and sold it to their neighbours. Alexander Russell then bought Aden estate.

The present owners of Montcoffer House are Alec and Dorothy Clark, a Yorkshire couple who acquired the property at the end of 1989. They have landscaped the grounds and run Montcoffer as a guest house. Inside the library is a huge mirror identical to one in Duff House. Back in the 1960s and 70s, when two successive owners lived on the farm, the house was unoccupied and the library was used to stack bales of straw. This act of desecration had one unexpected result — it saved the mirror from destruction.

The Clarks provide refreshments for walkers tramping up from Banff to see the Bridge of Alvah, an unusual high-arched bridge built by the Earl of Fife in 1772. Alan Clark showed me round the grounds, taking me to two octagonal larders at the back of the house, one for game, the other for fish. Then I made my way down the brae to the old bridge, which had greatly impressed Doctor Pratt. He wrote:

> The bridge forms the culminating point of one of the most lovely valleys of Buchan. On the one bank, the hanging woods of Montcoffer; on the other, the highly ornamented grounds of Duff House. The top of the arch is said to be nearly forty feet above the level of the stream. In the great flood of 1829 the water reached nearly to the apex, rushing through with indescribable fury.

On one side of the bridge a curious arch-shaped opening can be seen in the wall. It looks like a window, making you wonder if someone had actually lived *inside* the bridge. This, in fact, was where a room was built into the structure to accommodate a toll collector. The door, which is well below the parapet on the opposite side of the bridge, seems to be at an almost impossible point of entry.

There were no toll collectors when I crossed the bridge and made my way back through the Montcoffer woods by an old drove road that was to take me to Banff. Cattle, sheep and horses were once driven along this track. There were 'cadgers' rigs', special plots, cleared on each side of it so that drovers could graze their beasts when they broke their journey on the approach to Banff. There is still a link with those long-forgotten days in an old milestone half-hidden in the undergrowth at the side of the track.

The road ran down to the local distillery. Beyond it lay Banff Bridge — 'the Bonny Brig o' Banff' — and the wide sweep of the bay. I stood there thinking of Johnny Gibb of Gushetneuk, who on his way to the Wells at Macduff had come along the 'delightsome' road by Knockiemill and Eden and had looked out over the bay to see 'a brave schooner scudding along the Firth, with fully spread canvas'. Mary Howie, Mrs Gibb's niece, asked if they would get a sail on the water and was warned of the possibility of 'the boat coupin an' you gyaun to the boddom o' the sea'. If that didn't happen, she was told, it was certainly more than likely that she would be 'as deid's a door nail wi' sea sickness'.

The ferry crossing was bad enough, but the floods that tormented Banff and Macduff folk were worse. Floods swept away the first bridge over the Deveron five years after it was built in 1763. In 1780 it was replaced by John Smeaton's bridge. Long before that, when the waters burst in January, 1739, three men and three women, who were crossing the Deveron in the ferry boat, were swept down the river and out to sea. Two men and two of the women died. The third woman was saved because she had a large pack of wool on her back.

It acted as a buoy until a boat from Macduff reached her in the bay and picked her up.

When Johnny Gibb came down into Macduff his eye caught a street sign, Duff Street. 'Fat whigmaleerie's this noo?' he asked. 'The fowk o' this place wud ca' their vera tykes aifter the Earl o' Fife. This is fat we ees't to ca' the "Main Street". Duff Street; fat sorra ither!'

There are no dogs called 'aifter the Earl o' Fife' nowadays, or none, at any rate, that I know of, but the name of Duff is perpetuated in a dozen different ways along the Deveron, not least by the great baroque palace, Duff House, which dominates the approach to Banff. Built in the 1730s for William Duff, later Lord Braco and the first Earl of Fife, it has now become an outpost of the Scottish National Galleries in Edinburgh ... a Country House Gallery showing some 200 works from the national collection, while at the same time recreating the atmosphere of a great ducal house.

It was there that my journey through Buchan ended. It had taken me to the 'new' towns, to the farmlands where my forbears toiled, and to a coastline where 'the banshee sea wind raves'. I had wandered across the black peatlands of Buchan and chased my tail among the crofts of Clochforbie. I had seen where the lairds once lived in their great mansions, and where they lived now, clinging to their privileged past.

I sat in their shadow above the Bridge of Alvah, enjoying tea and crumpets on the sunlit lawn of Montcoffer House and thinking of the ancestral ghosts that were on my heels. For it was at Alvah on June 7th, 1878, that my grandfather, John Murdoch, and Agnes Munro, the grandmother I never knew, were married. Three years later my mother was born at Raecloch, Turriff, and baptised that December at the kirk at Marnoch, south of Foggieloan.

So that was it. I had come full circle. I had paid my respects to Mormond and tipped my hat to Aikey Brae. I had rediscovered the Land of Plenty.

Further Reading

Allan, John R., *The North-East Lowlands of Scotland*. Hale, 1952.

Alexander, William, *Rural Life in Victorian Aberdeenshire*. Mercat Press, 1992.

Carter, Ian, *Farm Life in North-east Scotland, 1840–1914*. John Donald, 1979.

Duffus, H. and S., A History of Monquhitter. Stanley Duffus, 1985.

Fenton, Alexander, *Wirds an' Wark 'e Seasons Roon*. Aberdeen University Press, 1987.

Godsman, James, *King Edward, The Story of a Parish*. Banffshire Journal, 1952.

Graham, Cuthbert, *Portrait of Aberdeen and Deeside*. Hale, 1972.

Marshall, Christian Watt, *A Stranger on the Bars*. Banff and Buchan District Council Leisure and Recreation Dept., 1994.

Milne, John C., *Poems*. Aberdeen University Press, 1963.

McWilliam, Rev. Thomas, *Sketch of a Quiet Buchan Parish*. Banff, 1899.

Pratt, John B., *Buchan*. Heritage Press, 1978.

Smith, Robert, *One Foot in the Sea*. John Donald, 1991.

Tranter, Nigel, *The Queen's Scotland*. Hodder and Stoughton, 1972.

Watt, Christian, *The Christian Watt Papers*, edited by General Sir David Fraser. Paul Harris, 1983.

Webster, Jack, *A Grain of Truth*. Paul Harris, 1981.

Wood, Sydney, *The Shaping of 19th Century Aberdeenshire*. Spa Books, 1985.

Index

INDEX